How Am I Supposed to Love Myself?

PHOEBE CRANOR

Bethany Fellowship INC.
MINNEAPOLIS, MINNESOTA 55438

Published by Bethany Fellowship, Inc.
6820 Auto Club Road, Minneapolis, Minnesota 55438

Printed in the United States of America

Cranor, Phoebe.
    How am I supposed to love myself?

    Includes index.
    1. Wives—Religious life.   2. Christian life—
1960-   3. Self-love (Theology)   I. Title.
BV4527.C72   248'.843   79-14229
ISBN 0-87123-236-7

Dedication

To the rest of the team: Jean, Kay, Madelaine, Marie,
Nancy, Peggy, Terry

PHOEBE CRANOR and her husband, who is a Colorado cattle rancher, have raised four children. She has had nineteen years' experience as a Sunday school teacher, and has taught one year in the Arizona public school system. She is presently active in an inner-healing prayer and counseling group.

Mrs. Cranor has a B.A. degree from the Arizona State University. Through the years, many of her stories, poems, and articles have been published, including four leaflets by Dove Publications, Pecos, New Mexico. Her first two books are *Why Did God Let Grandpa Die?*, Bethany Fellowship, 1976, and *Why Doesn't God Do Something?*, Bethany Fellowship, 1978.

Table of Contents

Preface

This book is a record of another section in my own spiritual journey, written for the purpose of sharing my insights with other travelers on the road toward wholeness in Christ Jesus. The Bible is my road map. Many people have asked me to make a statement about the way I approach Holy Scripture, so I will do that right here, first of all.

To begin with, I believe that the Bible, the inspired Word of God, is a trinity in itself. Initially it is God's Word *historically*. It was for and to and concerning the people who lived at the specific ages about which it was written. In order to understand what God was doing in the lives of those people, we need to learn as much of their history and philosophies as we can.

Second, I believe that the Bible is totally *prophetic*. It has in it everything that ever was and is and is to be. God's whole picture of mankind, from beginning to end, is in the Bible; whatever has not yet happened is bound, still, to take place so that the wholeness of man's place in the entirety of creation will be completed.

Third, I believe that Holy Scripture is God's *personal letter* (love letter, in fact) written to each individual He has ever created. My life is there, along with yours and yours and even yours. If I have a need, its answer lies in the Bible. If I have a question, a hurt, a joy, I can find response to it by reading God's Word. If a statement rings true to Scripture, even though it is in the language of science or math or psychology or some other language not even yet invented, then I can accept it because I also read and believe the Word of God.

I see in my own life a microcosm of the whole Bible. Just as the first man, at Creation, I begin in innocence and grow to choose self instead of God. I serve self. In fact, I am nearly destroyed in a great flood of selfishness. I go into captivity; but I am led out again. I spend time in the wilderness, first turning toward and then again away from the God who is my Father. Finally I am through the wilderness and reach the Promised Land. Only it isn't all I thought it would be. I want judges. I want kings. I fall away and return. I live in periodic slavery, war, and misery. Still, all through my ages, I catch now and then a prophetic vision of the Christ to come. I know there is something more, always something more.

Although I live in the terrible bondage of some sort of legalism, I am finally aware that my Saviour has at last arrived. I go through all the stages of joy and doubt, of witnessing miracles, of running away, of being the traitor. Suddenly my Lord is gone. I am in despair. I am sure that He has died forever. The burden of life is too great to endure. Then, after an agonizing period, I have my own Easter. The historical Christ becomes a personal Christ. He is born again in my heart, and I am *new*. I am redeemed from sin, from selfishness, from eternal death! I have seen Love in Person and He is enough; I sit at His feet until He tells me that He will come in a new way again, this time in power that will transform my life.

When it comes, my life is indeed transformed. I realize that love is, in truth, the only thing that is of importance. Everything that has happened since the Garden of Eden has been for the moment when love triumphs. I am filled with the Spirit and feel endlessly joyful! He is with me and in me.

Life, though, isn't the perfection I want it to be. I have trials, persecution, even denials. I learn more clearly all the while that even though love is the focus, I am less than mature; with each faltering step I learn to put my foot down more firmly. I work and fail and try again. I grow until finally I am ready with Saint John to say nothing more than, "Come, Lord Jesus."

Where are you, friend? Are you in the Old Testament or the New? Are you back in the wilderness or fighting with Paul against the Roman persecution? Are you tired? The important fact is that wherever you are, He is. His love is all-encompassing. He waits through our darkness for each one of us just as He is waiting (and working while He waits) for the completion of His plan. The little one who has not yet left the Garden of Innocence is precious to Him. The one still groping about in the wilderness is of infinite value. And imagine His joy when that one opens his heart to the Saviour! And when that one completes his journey, the Saviour is there with open arms to welcome him Home.

God loves me whether I succeed or fail; He loves me if I am in rebellion. I don't want to rebel. I want to please my Father. I want to be perfect for Him and for myself. But it doesn't matter, where His love is concerned, what

I do or don't do. Love is God and God is Love. His love is bigger than all evil. Surely a love that big, that strong, can lift me out of every darkness, within and without.

Chapter 1

Please Pass the Wastebasket

How can I get rid of old hang-ups?

"You'll just have to decide to get rid of all those old magazines," my husband told me firmly when we were ready to move into our new house. It was a thirty-year accumulation of one of the popular monthly magazines; and I had saved every issue. I could hardly bear the idea, yet I knew that even though there were undoubtedly some things in the magazines worth saving, I would certainly have to eliminate them in order for us to fit into a smaller home.

Parting with merely the sheer bulk of 360 magazines was hard, even if they were of no value. Bulk is often a very secure item in an insecure world. The space where they had been would surely look empty. I hedged. Maybe I could keep just a few? Maybe I could sort through them and find ones I really wanted? I had never looked at them twice in the entire thirty years. Yes, Lord. My husband is right.

So I struggled up the basement stairs carrying as many as I could in my arms. As I staggered out of the dark celler into the sunshine of the backyard, my arms were so filled with dusty old magazines that I could hardly see the sun. And I couldn't see the porch step at all. Suddenly I was sprawled amid a mountain of paper all over the east side of the house. Lord, whatever are you telling me? There is more than half a ton of magazines here.

After I quit teaching Sunday school, I became part of a small team of women who focus a great deal of time and energy praying for inner healing from old hurting memories buried deep in all of our past lives. We have found that our experiences often are not "remembered" memories. They are, all the same, feeling parts of what we become as adults. Even hidden away, as they are when their pain is too intense, they have their effect on us just as a bit of walled-off infection can poison our bodies. As our team learned how best to pray for each other, we began to experience tremendous change in our own lives. The light of the presence of Jesus began to permeate the hurt places and heal them. We found new joy, love, talent, capacity, and compassion. After a time, the Lord began to send people to us for prayer. They, too, experienced new freedom. Jesus did come to give release to the captives (Luke 4:18), and He is doing that no less now than He did two thousand years ago. Never mind whether the prisons are outside, with walls of stone or barbed wire, or inside, with walls of forgetfulness. He is still able to break them down.

Time truly means nothing to Jesus. The past or the future are no barrier to Him: not space nor place nor circumstance. He knew us before we were formed in our mothers' wombs. He wants our wholeness and our perfection. When He said, "Be perfect [whole, complete] as your Father in heaven is perfect," He wasn't making a tea-party observation. That was a command. He is telling me personally that He will go to all lengths to give me the healing and the assistance to fulfill that command. He isn't finished with me yet. But I do know that I have seen a great change in my own inner self since I began asking Him for His presence in the painful places in my past.

I told my friends on the team about my magazine disposal efforts. I asked them, "Do you think the Lord was giving me something with that episode?" We sat in silence, pondering. I began to see that I had been locked into a limitation made up of old ideas. It seemed that a lot of my creative energy was bound into unused volumes, quite covered with dust. Their bulk obscured my vision, causing me to fail to see my way, even when the sun was shining. When I fell, they were scattered and I was free to wonder what new message was coming into my life. I began to laugh. Jesus, the light of the world, was giving me a big object lesson, and I was just starting to grasp its meaning.

As we discussed what limitations we had been putting on our vision with leftover tomes from the past, we began to "see" what seemed to be a giant wastebasket, as if the Lord had sent it with the command that we each put into it some limiting idea from our own store. We went around the circle seeing, identifying, and expressing our willingness to be rid of some specific pre-formed limitation. We laughed and we cried; and we emerged with a knowledge of His presence so warm that we knew this was no moment of fantasy. Since that day, the holy wastebasket has been a constant part of our group. One of the angels must empty it every evening, otherwise I'm sure by now it would be heaped to overflowing with the many inhibitions and prohibitions we have imposed on the magnificence of God.

For that is what we began to see—that day when the basket first arrived: we have concocted stacks of words and ideas and bound them in the storehouses of our minds. These keep us from experiencing the wonder and glory of God's love. Over and over again we have stifled Him in our lives and the lives of others. And, because He has given us free choice as a part of our birthright, He lets us go on limiting Him until we decide on our own to stop. We, of the inner healing team, received a vision of the possibility of discarding those restrictions which we had always put on God, our Father—Creator and the source of all that was and is and ever will be.

Since that day, we have been inviting our friends and those who come asking for help and prayer to add to the contents of the wide-open basket. Sometimes it is a tremendous relief to be rid of a burdensome smallness. But other times it is equally painful to lay aside a much-used crutch. People definitely are not always interested in new insights. Fear and habit and lack of love in many lives inhibit the emergence of new possibilities—even new dimensions of the love and forgiveness of God.

The team has learned to pray for a long time for each person who comes into our prayer focus and never, never, *never* to rush inner-healing prayer onto him before he himself asks for it. We have learned that even after first and second and third sessions of prayer for the relief of old hurts, there are habits and matters that have to be dealt with by the continuing action of the Holy Spirit. All we can do is keep praying and loving, not judging, not condemning—and most of all continue to ask for the elimination of our own hang-ups.

One day there was a knock on my door. As I opened it, I was almost overwhelmed by the defensiveness of a woman whom I knew only slightly.

"I came to tell you that this 'inner healing' business is all wrong! It isn't scriptural. When we accept Jesus, we are to become new beings with no more sin in us. You people are saying that we can blame our sins on our parents. No! We must forget the past and root ourselves in our Lord. That is all false doctrine and you are false prophets talking heresy!"

The stern gray-haired lady confronted me, Bible in hand, her disapproval pouring generously down on me from her five-inch greater height. Before I had experienced the real power of the Lord Jesus' healing touch, I would have been completely immobilized by the authority and displeasure in her voice. I would have burbled pointlessly, my words barely audible over the pounding of my heart. And I would have been defenseless and furious for days and nights afterward.

But the power to free prisoners, this power that Jesus accepted for himself from the prophecy of Isaiah, had truly been happening to me. The initial hurt, the debilitating terror from anyone who spoke with authority, had been healed. And the habit of behaving as if I were still afraid was—and still is—being taken care of. Instead of cowering before this emphatic lady, I saw her as a person threatened by new ideas, a person haunted by the need to have a sure-fire rule for every situation and to kill quickly any situation that didn't fit her rules. Compassion filled me. My own blocks were out of the way enough so that I could allow the Spirit to speak in my defense—if defense it was. Perhaps, instead, it was the beginning of a learning situation for a frightened old woman.

So I inwardly asked, deliberately throwing away my own old habits, "As You did for me when I was teaching children younger in years but no less developed in grace, please, Holy Spirit, speak to this woman with my voice."

* * * * *

If a parent dropped his five-day-old baby on the floor, damaging its brain so badly that it remained forever afterward a helpless cripple, we would have no hesitation in saying that the person is in his sorry condition because of his injury. Physical damage can cause retarded mental and physical development. Although the years pass and the child becomes older, he stays in nearly the same place mentally because of the old injury. Perhaps he is also physically handicapped, maybe never learning to walk or to take care of his simplest needs for himself. We understand that all of these things are the result of a bad fall when he was five days old.

An injury to a baby's emotions can result from any one of a number of very early traumas, and he can very well grow up physically and mentally while remaining emotionally retarded because he has never recovered from the injury. While the whole world can see the results of a physical injury, an emotional one often is harder to spot. All the same, the person who is so emotionally behind can no more be called responsible for his condition than the one who was dropped on his head and had his brain damaged.

Scientists and psychiatrists often can discover the results of emotional hurts that occurred in our childhood; but they are not always available with their skills, nor are they always successful in the treatment of them even when they are there to help. Just as doctors at times can do nothing at all for the retarded, brain-damaged child, so many times psychiatric doctors are helpless before the damage inflicted on the emotional life of a person. Neither of these conditions can fairly be labeled "sin." They do not excuse sin nor do they cause it. They don't preclude it. They are just "horses of a different color." To deal with injury the same way as one deals with sin is not scriptural, either. Jesus healed, forgave, cast out demons. He cured the hurt in the area where the hurt existed.

Not only was He the greatest physician in the world, Jesus was also the greatest psychiatrist. He knew at once what to say to reach the person that would touch the troubled center. One man had to come to terms with wealth. Another had to decide whether or not he really wanted healing. The deaf mute was so damaged that all Jesus required of him was to come away from the crowd and receive the touch of wholeness.

We all know that people are made up of more than just the physical body. The Bible calls the different parts body, soul and spirit. These larger classifications can be broken down still further: mind, will, emotion, body, and spirit. When we accept the Lord Jesus into our lives, our spirits do indeed become immediately new. But even Paul realized that "what I want to do, I don't do, and what I don't want to do, I still go on doing." Our spirits can become new without automatically bringing into newness the old mental and emotional problems left over from the days before we even had formed the concepts to remember them.

For example, supposing a man is afraid of dogs. He masks his fear under the guise of anger—anger at whoever has a dog and at everything the dog does. The man becomes a Christian. His life is drastically changed in many areas, but he doesn't change in his attitude toward dogs. His anger is controlled. He doesn't fight with his dog-owning neighbors. But he still will not consider letting his children have a dog.

One day the man finds a friend who prays with him for the healing of all his old memories, and one of the memories that comes to his mind is of being badly hurt and frightened by a dog once long, long ago. As he relives that memory, he asks Jesus to take away that fear at its source, to heal the initial experience with dogs that started his whole lifetime of bad feelings toward them. As that happens, he sees that he has given a new part of himself into the loving hands of the Lord. Sooner or later, depending upon how fast he is able to get rid of his habits of behavior, the man will first allow his children a puppy and then, finally, learn to appreciate dogs himself. Much of life is habit. We must first be healed of the original hurt and then day-by-day be aware of and willing to be rid of the habits the old pain caused.

Before we accept Jesus as Saviour, there is no good way to reach and heal the deep hurts which we have experienced in the long-ago past. So they can continue to dictate our behavior without relief. Then Jesus walks in, and with Him comes unlimited possibilities. The old is made new? Of course. We only have to recognize that we can now participate in a newness of which we never before had even the barest glimpse.

Because every experience we ever have had is still with us in the hidden rooms of the subconscious, the way to deal with any of our painful memories is to find them and hold them out for Jesus to heal. This is easier said than done, for nothing forms a bigger, more impenetrable block against love than a long-ago terror. Where I have been hurt, I refuse to allow a trespasser, even if the "trespasser" is the Lord Jesus himself. Often I do not know that I have refused. Only as I realize how much my old hurts are dictating my present behavior do I accept Jesus' invitation to allow His light to shine in and dispel my own inner darkness.

Scripture

" . . . he draws me from deep waters, he delivers me from my powerful enemy, from a foe too strong for me" (Ps. 18:16-17).

"What God can compare with you: taking fault away, pardoning crime, not cherishing anger forever, but delighting in showing mercy?" (Mic. 7:18-19).

"He stood up to read, and they handed him the scroll of the prophet Isaiah. Unrolling the scroll he found the place where it is written:

'The spirit of the Lord has been given to me,
for he has anointed me.
He has sent me to bring the good news to the poor,

22

to proclaim liberty to captives
and to the blind new sight,
to set the downtrodden free,
to proclaim the Lord's year of favor.'
He then rolled up the scroll, gave it back to the assistant
and sat down. And all eyes in the synagogue were fixed
on him. Then he began to speak to them, 'This text is being fulfilled today even as you listen' " (Luke 4:17-21).

"So no matter who you are, if you pass judgment you
have no excuse" (Rom. 2:1).

"Yes, we were carrying our own death warrant with
us, and it has taught us not to rely on ourselves but only
on God, who raises the dead to life. And he saved us from
dying, as he will save us again; yes that is our firm hope
in him, that in the future he will save us again" (2 Cor.
1:9-11).

Chapter 2

A Basket of Bubbles

How am I supposed to love myself?

"I think this inner healing stuff is entirely too self-centered. We are supposed to forget ourselves—to die to self and love and serve our fellowman. Concentration on what's inside of us just makes us introverts and takes our attention away from working for the Lord."

This time my critic was a man. He was admittedly a conscientious and prolific worker, doing as hard and as fast as he could whatever he saw that needed doing. He had the admiration of the community—with the possible exception of a few people who felt railroaded by his arbitrary methods. He pulled out his Bible and read some of the admonitions that fit what he was telling me. I knew I had had to deal with those things myself, once, so I could listen to him.

There was another reason I could listen, though. Once I was afraid and suspicious of men. I came from a long line of women who did not like men (and probably

also did not like the masculine part of themselves). I
grew up mistrusting, generally, anything that came from
a male. In spite of a good husband and a fine son, I could
not change my feelings. But Jesus could; and He did. A
man whom I barely knew prayed for me one evening after
a prayer meeting. As he prayed, his hand on my shoulder, the heat from his palm seemed to flow through me to
the very soles of my feet. I began to cry. For half an hour
the tears poured out until, alone in the half-dark room, I
felt as washed as a baby after a bath. I knew something
had happened, but I had no idea what it was until later
when I remembered that my friend had asked Jesus to
walk back into my life and touch it in the places where I
needed Him most. I knew where I needed Him at that
point. I had figured out that my antipathy toward men
was inhibiting my relationship with Jesus, who is, after
all, a man. In order to know and love Him to the fullest
extent of my capacity, I realized that I must first recover
from that old, old hurt which had made me think that
men are awful creatures.

Facing this man, apparently a self-confident man at
that, I was aware that my old scar tissue did indeed con-
tain a new strength. I could see him taking one small
fearful peek into the depths of his own pain and being too
frightened to look again. I could see him running from
one important job to another, doing "the Lord's work" to
keep from knowing his own person. It had never occurred
to him that he was serving the Lord incidentally while
busily serving the little boy inside of himself who kept
saying, "I've gotta prove to my daddy that I am a good
boy so he'll love me." Jesus knew. He stood by, willing to
help if so much as a hint came along that my friend
would let Him. Could I tell the suffering child inside this

grown man that it wouldn't be fatal to look at his pain and then offer it to Him who heals all pain? Not by myself, I couldn't. So I took a deep breath and turned my lips over to the Spirit to speak whatever words of wisdom He wanted through me.

* * * * *

Imagine a little boy with a favorite possession: a pretty basket. He carries all sorts of small treasures about in it, emptying it periodically to put in something else. One evening he is helping his mother wash the dishes, doing, as is common to all small children, more playing with the soapsuds than dish washing.

All at once our little boy realizes that he has made a mountain of beautiful bubbles. They float high above the dishpan and mound in colorful heaps under his hands. His father is sitting in the living room reading his newspaper and the little boy thinks of a wonderful idea. He gathers up all the frothy soapsuds that his basket will hold and runs to his father with them.

"See, Daddy, I have brought you a present! It is so pretty. Hear the bubbles pop and see the color. Daddy, this basket of bubbles is all yours. You can do whatever you want with them."

Daddy, being a loving and understanding father, accepts the basket of bubbles graciously, realizing that this is the best thing his child has to offer him. But it isn't until many, many years later that the little-boy-grown-up realizes what a useless gift his basket of soap bubbles really was. It was surface and shiny. It was moving. But what, after all, could Daddy really do with the bubbles? The warm water under the bubbles might have had any one of several uses. But the froth on top soon turned to nothing.

God, our understanding Father, will accept with grace whatever we give Him. If we give Him the surface of our lives, however shiny and active, He will take it and thank us gravely. But much of what we do with this frothy topping for the deep water underneath will vanish as bubbles in the air. What God would like is for us to dig under the surface and give Him whatever is real. It may not look like anything good to us. God knows better. He created us. He loves us. Whatever is inside is totally known to Him. He accepts us as we are. That is the reason for the death of Jesus on the cross. There is no longer a chasm between what is inside of us and our Creator. It is gone because Jesus gave His life to remove it. If I am hiding my inner self from someone, that someone isn't God. It is most likely only me.

*   *   *   *   *

Again the wastebasket moved into the midst of a situation. What old hang-ups, what preconceived notion, could be discarded from the man's consciousness? To begin with, we needed to discard the idea that it is not in line with Christ's teachings to spend time and effort in knowing ourselves. When He gave the commandment to love God with all of our potential and to love our neighbors as ourselves, He was telling us two things. One is that if we "love" ourselves by hating ourselves, we will love our neighbors the same way. In order to follow His commandment, we must eliminate that hatred. Usually one ceases to fear and hate that which he truly understands.

To love is to listen and to listen is to love. When I have learned to listen to myself, the why of me and the how of me, then I will begin to feel a deep love for myself. At that point I will be able to listen to and love my neighbor. My own experience with a suspicious hatred for men is a good example. I used to approach any man with prejudice. I listened to only the things he said which reinforced my prejudice. After I discovered, acknowledged, and finally was healed of my dislike of men, I found I could really hear the person behind the words—even when that person was male. And, hearing him, I could minister the love of God to him where his needs existed.

The other thing I think Jesus was telling us was that we cannot love God to any depth with an unknown self. He said that we should love Him with *all* our hearts and souls and minds and might and thoughts and feelings. If I never have met *all* of me, how can I love with *all* of me? Before I can fulfill that commandment, I must know something of who I am and why I am and how I am— then I can knowingly give my gift to my Lord. Giving my frantic activity, my surface movements, my busyness, is like the child giving his daddy his bubbles. It is really a very useless gift.

I am not saying that God can't ever use soap bubbles—frantic busy work or self-centered activity. Nothing is impossible to Him. But if I can know and love myself, then I can participate with Him in what He is doing. I think that is a part of the Kingdom, ultimately: to be a co-creator with our Father who created us. I want to willingly give Him every part of me, from the "best" on through to what I consider (and maybe He doesn't) the "worst," so I can be a part of whatever He is doing.

Jesus told us to seek first the Kingdom of God and then all else would come along in its proper time. He also told us that the Kingdom of God is in, among, and with us. We don't go seeking the Kingdom in some faraway place. Instead we find it, as the bluebird of happiness,

28

right where we are. He is here. He said so. "I will never leave you nor forsake you," He told us. The uncommon country of our inner selves is His territory, and we can take part in the exploration and development of it. When Jesus said, "As a man thinks in his heart, so he is," He was telling us that if we are full of fear, hate, prejudice—any kind of garbage—these dictate our behavior. We do not love either ourselves or our neighbors. Come, Holy Spirit, and help us to recognize the bubbles for what they are and look beneath them to our real selves. And then, Lord, carry away the trash that keeps us from loving our neighbor as ourself.

Scripture

"Yahweh is looking down from heaven at the sons of men, to see if a single one is wise, if a single one is seeking God" (Ps. 14:2).

"I bless Yahweh, who is my counselor, and in the night my inmost self instructs me" (Ps. 16:7).

" . . . since what I want is love, not sacrifice; knowledge of God, not holocausts" (Hos. 6:6).

"You did not choose me, no, I chose you; and I commissioned you to go out and to bear fruit" (John 15:16).

"Failing to recognize the righteousness that comes from God, they try to promote their own idea of it, instead of submitting to the righteousness of God. But now the Law has come to an end with Christ, and everyone who has faith may be justified" (Rom. 10:3-4).

"I am quite certain that the One who began this good work in you will see that it is finished when the Day of Christ Jesus comes" (Phil. 1:6).

Chapter 3

Old English and a Straitjacket

Should I act more "spiritual" than I really am in order to be a good witness for the Lord?

My dear lawyer friend looked a bit pale and drawn. "What's wrong?" I asked him.

"An ulcer," he responded. I was truly surprised. He had come into a knowledge of Jesus as his Lord and Saviour and had overflowed with joy for the first six-month honeymoon. He had never had an ulcer before. He had never even been really ill before, as far as I knew. Jesus hardly would do that to him. Jesus is the light of the world, ultimately bringing peace and joy and health. Something else had caused it. I prayed silently before questioning him further.

It seemed that my friend had a hot and impetuous nature, full of temper and tenderness. At first he had been overcome with such a rush of joy that all of his responses were happy. Finally, though, as often happens after the first glowing days, the hard realities of life began to show again. He was new in the Lord, but he was still himself. However, as he read the Bible he felt that he was supposed to have changed his way of doing things altogether. From impetuous and hot tempered, he felt he should have gone immediately to gentle and thoughtful. Moreover, he felt that if he hadn't, he would hurt his "witness to what the Lord had done in his life." He was suddenly catapulted into a game of repressing his nature, no matter what, "for the sake of the Lord."

It wasn't the first time that I had heard this kind of thinking expressed. Some people spend all of their lives and the lives of their children (as long as they can) trying to maintain their "witness." My friend, though, was particularly blessed: the Lord had let him have an ulcer to show him the error of his ways.

But how can I tell him that? What will make him listen to anything that seems to spell *not* being a "good witness for the Lord?" Holy Spirit, I need some words for this man who is so enthusiastic for his Lord and Master.

* * * * *

Imagine a man who has been injured and is forced to wear a cast from his chin to his knees. To stave off his boredom, he has accepted a friend's invitation to a party. Someone brings him to the party after it is well under way, and when he arrives there is lots of laughing and merrymaking.

When our handicapped friend arrives at the party, the other guests gather around him. They tell him how glad they are that he came and they hope he has a good time. However, most of them are just a trifle uncomfortable continuing in their unrestrained good time, because they can see him lying there on his pallet not able to move. They mill about for a few minutes in some confusion and then gather around him. They begin to talk and share their own experiences with being "out of things." Although the party has taken a new turn, it promises still to be a good party. People are frank and open and ready to let their hair down, inspired by the unusual condition of one of the guests.

Supposing, though, that instead of joining in the conversation with freedom and openness, our crippled guest insists upon speaking nothing but old English. The stilted sound of that almost-foreign tongue, along with the enforced oddity of his other behavior, stops all conversation immediately. Nobody knows just what to do and finally some of the guests make an excuse and leave. Before long the party has broken up.

Now, Christianity is not a straitjacket and its language is not a foreign one. But some people by the stilted and unbending way they go about their "Christian witness" give exactly that impression. Why? Because they are not being truthful. A witness on the stand in a courtroom must promise to tell the truth, the whole truth, and nothing but the truth. A witness for Christ is to do the same thing. He is not to play lawyer and try to prove something or play judge and decide what is to happen; he is not even to play jury and give a verdict. All he is to do is tell the truth—what, exactly, has happened to him.

A person who dons a costume and a mask and calls it "Christian" is not telling the whole truth, nor is he telling nothing but the truth. He is, instead, acting out a lie. Certainly the way we live our lives is a witness to what Christ has done in them. But it is not achieved by what we can do by ourselves.

Then what, you ask, *is* a Christian's "witness"? What

responsibility do we have? The answer, I believe, comes from the inside first. When we accept Jesus, we are filled with a new potential to love. Because He died to redeem us from sin, self and the devil—to heal our alienation from God—we are truly new as soon as we ask Him into our lives. We are new in spirit. He has transformed that innermost spirit into a likeness of himself. Our motives, attitudes and values are totally transformed. Yes, in spite of its misuse today, Jesus' phrase "born again" describes this change. But we still have the same bodies, and intellects, the same knowledge, and even some of the same hang-ups, bad habits, and peculiarities of personality that we always had. We most likely have some dark hurting secrets that we are not even aware exist. By ourselves we are not able to put these things off all at once and become completely different.

So what we do is *grow* into His likeness. As a baby learns to walk—taking a step, swaying, falling down and getting back up—a new Christian will need to be trained by the Holy Spirit in this new walk. The whole truth is that my friend still has the habit of a hot temper and a sensitive nature. Acting as if he doesn't is only his human response to the problem; it is also destroying his insides.

What we must do, instead of putting on masks, is to start at the center of our beings by asking Jesus to guide and direct and heal and be present in such a real way that whenever anyone meets one of us, he senses that the Other is present also. That is not acting. Instead it is a great commitment that allows the love of God to go into new and unknown places deep in the subconscious. In that way, whatever changes take place are so real, so natural (or should we say *supernatural*), that they are almost unnoticed.

Did Jesus act a part? Of course not. He was *himself*. Being God as well as man, that Self was without flaw. But if we are to take a cue from Him, we will see that He witnessed of the Father by living His life in total honesty and openness. What He was, He was. He was also sensitive. He was hurt and disappointed. He sighed. He slipped away to rest and pray. He was those ways because He was meant to be. His anger was for the purpose of coming against evil. His sensitivity was for the purpose of "knowing what was in their hearts"; His tenderness was for all those lost and apart from His Father who loves them all. He was disappointed at lack of faith in His followers.

It is easy to get an ulcer when we are wearing a cast and speaking old English. There is no in-and-out-flow of the Spirit, only repression and pretending and stiffness. But if we are aware of a new and wonderful Friend living with us not only on the outside but in us at the very heart of things, then our witness is easy. It amounts to saying with our actions:

"Meet my Friend. He loves me just as I am. Because He first loved me without reservation, I am beginning to see that I can love you that same way. I am a person with a hot temper. So I have given it to my Lord and am watching to see how He will temper it. Whenever I feel that I have grabbed it back and used it wrongly, I am able to tell Him that I have. I then ask His forgiveness, and pray that He will redeem whatever has happened. I am becoming comfortable with the knowledge that 're-demption' isn't just once and for all, but is minute by minute."

That kind of a Christian witness is believable. It allows the Holy Spirit to speak through me to the parti-cular need in another person without my having to turn myself inside out doing or being what I have decided a Christian is supposed to do and be.

My father was an instructor at the Phoenix Indian School. When I was a child, we lived at the end of the street where trash was dumped and periodically burned. I used to love to go there and hunt through piles of inter-esting government-red-tape sorts of things: forms and requisition blanks and attendance records and many un-used "goodies" whose purposes must have been forgotten before they were printed. I saved handfuls of the most in-triguing ones to play with later. Since I played alone most of the time, I spent hours happily pretending as I filled them out. I had not only saved those little pieces of paper *from* destruction, I had saved them *for* something creative.

When Jesus died on the cross to save us from our sins, the strong implication, I think, was that we had been saved, like my happy little papers, also for something creative. I was made for a purpose, and I was saved for a purpose. Instead of acting a part, I had better get on with finding out how I can cooperate with my reason for be-ing. I had better quickly discard my act and my mask and my foreign language and get on with being the new *me*.

Scripture

"Free your neck from its fetters, captive daughter of Zion" (Isa. 52:2).

"But for you who fear my name, the sun of righteousness will shine out with healing in its rays; you will leap like calves going out to pasture" (Mal. 3:16).

"Alas for you, scribes and Pharisees, you hypocrites! You who pay your tithe of mint and dill and cummin and have neglected the weightier matters of the Law—justice, mercy, good faith! These you should have practiced, without neglecting the others" (Matt. 23:23).

"Do not model yourselves on the behavior of the world around you, but let your behavior change, modeled by your new mind. This is the only way to discover the will of God and know what is good, what it is that God wants, what is the perfect thing to do" (Rom. 12:2)

" . . . and where the Spirit of the Lord is, there is freedom. And we, with our unveiled faces reflecting like mirrors the brightness of the Lord, all grow brighter and brighter as we are turned into the image that we reflect; this is the work of the Lord who is Spirit" (2 Cor. 3:18).

Chapter 4

The IRS Man Has Arrived

How can I be a submissive wife without burying my God-given personality?

"I hope I haven't kept you waiting."

The young woman who stepped into my living room was elegant—tall and graceful, stylishly dressed, hair thick and beautifully coiffed. She was the kind of lady before whom, a few years ago, I would have fallen over my feet in choking embarrassment, hurriedly telling her whatever good I could think of about myself to compensate for the fact that she was everything I wasn't. Instead, that day I waved her to a space on the rug and handed her a cup of coffee, watching as she gracefully folded her long legs. She was not in my living room by any accident. The Lord had sent her because she needed something that He would allow to come through me. So I looked, not at her style and beauty, but into her eyes.

There I saw a little girl crying out for love, pleading for help.

"Tell me," I invited, curling up beside her on the carpet.

"My husband and I are both Christians," she began. "We accepted Christ after we had been married a few years. Ever since then I have tried to be a submissive wife and live as I was instructed. But now . . . " It was hard for her to go on. I waited. Finally she resumed her story. It seemed that suddenly she could no longer be the "perfect submissive wife." She began to do things she neither liked nor approved of. She felt guilty. Besides that, her husband, while never being exactly unfaithful, all the same gave every impression that he was more interested in less Christian, more exciting females. I prodded.

"What do you think attracted your husband to you before you were married?" She admitted that it was her spunk, her independence, her open expression of whatever she was feeling at the time.

"And now he doesn't like me and I don't blame him. I don't like myself." Suddenly the pleading little girl took over, tears spilled, and for a long time there was nothing but the grace of God's gift of freshly washed territory in which to begin asking Jesus for help.

When I taught Sunday school I learned that it is the Holy Spirit who tells a child what He wants that child to hear. After a lot of years of practicing the art of asking Him, I had finally learned that He would send me a story to fit the moment's need—a "what if . . . " or a "supposing that . . . " kind of story that my children would understand.

"Lord, send me a story for my elegant grown-up little girl," I asked silently. Aloud I heard my voice saying, "Perhaps we'd better begin with a question: what is a 'submissive wife'?" I'm sure my friend was no more surprised at the way the Holy Spirit answered that question than I was.

* * * * *

Supposing the IRS man calls you up and tells you that he wants you to submit all of your papers of every kind for the past year for him to look at. You might do what he asked in either of two ways. You might gather every paper into a big bundle, being careful to put all the things you think he might not like in the center of the bundle, well hidden by the more pleasant papers. Then you could lay the bundle on the floor, tied carefully so nothing would slip out, and invite the IRS man to walk on it. That would be one way to submit your papers to him.

However, I think he might not be entirely enthusiastic about that method of submission. He might very well prefer that you should lay each tiniest paper out on the table where he could see it and evaluate it. To "submit" means to lay out for inspection. Submitting yourself to your husband in a bundle with the "bad things" tucked inside and asking him to walk on it is no more what the Lord Jesus wants you to do than it is what the IRS inspector would like (and neither would your husband!).

Jesus came to make us whole. When He gave the command, "Be ye perfect [whole, complete] as your Father in heaven is perfect [whole, complete]," He did not say to be whole only if you are male. The woman has always been as much a part of Jesus' love and concern as the man. He does not want you to submit in any self-defeating way. If you present yourself to your husband in an open manner and he, as head of the household, accepts his Christian responsibility to love you as he loves his own body, then he will do what Jesus does: he will help you to develop your wholeness, investigating and nurturing every facet of the self that God created you to be.

*   *   *   *   *

My friend looked at me in awe, aware, as I was, that the message had come from God. It was as if our giant wastebasket had descended from heaven to the floor between us and she was being invited to deposit a big load of error in it. We both felt that she had been offered a fresh new start for a marriage that had begun in love and was not going to end. We began to pray that she could be freed from this limiting view of submission and healed of the repression of her true self which it had caused.

As we prayed I sensed a new mood, a feeling of fear. Of course we were treading on fresh territory. From the beginning of her Christian life, she had tried to follow the pattern of a submissive wife that she and many others had devised out of their own understanding. Now Someone was asking her to enlarge and perhaps even change that understanding. Would God be offended? Was she doing rightly? Again I prayed silently for guidance.

There is a child inside of each one of us—a hurt child who has hidden himself away from further pain. Maybe one of the things Jesus meant when He said, "Unless you turn around and become as little children, you can never enter the kingdom of God," was that in adulthood we must deliberately turn back to those hurt times and ask for the "Him" of that kingdom to come inside and heal. In any case, I asked quickly for something to give her in her fear of the growing that is a necessary part of becoming whole.

The Spirit was gentle. He showed us that when we first become Christians, we are new persons in a fresh situation. We don't have a great many inner guidelines to follow. So, as babies anywhere, we must be led and protected from the outside. God gave His "children of Israel" many specifications. We still have those, in addition to the ones which were implied or spoken by Jesus as He walked the earth and brought people to Him. We must learn them and find out how they work. These written regulations are like a playpen to a young child, a circumscribing of our limits.

But one of the elements of birth is growth. We are born to grow. A baby soon outgrows his playpen, no longer needing it because he has his own knowledge from his own observations. The specifications, the "rules," are still valid, but their application to one's life comes from within rather than from without. When God says, "You shall not steal," it does not mean merely that I should not take my playmate's toy but that I should not steal away my neighbor's reputation. We still need the direct guidance of the Word of God, of course; but our increasing spiritual understanding of the nature of God means that obedience will come out of love, not legalism.

So now my friend was outgrowing her "childish" interpretation of submission. "You no longer fit in the narrow confines of your playpen," I told (no, the Spirit told) her. "A new definition of submission allows you to grow into the person God created you to be. It allows you to recognize, deal with, and accept yourself as you are. Best of all, it allows you a new freedom which will soon show in your relationship with your husband, not in rebellion but in *mature* submission. Now you can go back to being the independent, spunky woman he fell in love with. You can do it knowing that Jesus Christ walks beside you and in you and that you are His growing-up disciple. You can do it without guilt or fear because you are basing your actions not on rules alone but on the greater 'rule' of love."

Scripture

"Now both of them were naked, the man and his wife, but they felt no shame in front of each other" (Gen. 2:25).

"Commit your fate to Yahweh, trust in him and he will act" (Ps. 37:5).

"I am a wall, and my breasts represent its towers. Under his eyes I have found true peace" (Song of Sol. 8:9b).

"And he replied, 'Did you never read what David did in his time of need when he and his followers were hungry—how he went into the house of God when Abiathar was high priest, and ate the loaves of offering which only the priests were allowed to eat, and how he also gave some to the men with him?'

"And he said to them, 'The sabbath was made for man, not man for the sabbath; so the Son of Man is master even of the sabbath' " (Mark 2:25-28).

"But now we are rid of the Law, freed by death from our imprisonment, free to serve in the new spiritual way and not the old way of a written law" (Rom. 7:6).

Chapter 5

A Raisin in the Soup

*Should I try to "protect" those close to me
from problems?*

"I'm ashamed to be back again so soon."

My lovely friend hadn't learned yet that inner
changes take time, just as the recovery from surgery
takes time—just as *any* growing up takes more than a
week. I welcomed her back. Her eyes were heavy with a
new kind of despair. What this time, my dear?

It seems that when she opened herself to her husband
as she had often done before they both became Christians, he felt threatened and became defensive. He expressed his anger vehemently and his hurt loudly. His
wife was afraid that she had no right to do that to him.

"I might hurt him. I couldn't do that," she wailed.

Holy Spirit, You guided my words last week. What is
wrong? Did we not hear You correctly? I waited in silent
prayer for a picture or a story to rescue the situation.

* * * * *

Supposing you entered an auditorium where a dozen jugglers were practicing their acts. One man was juggling five heavy iron skillets and one was juggling eighteen golf balls. One had seven bowling pins. One had plates. Another had wheels. Everyone was working so hard that there was no conversation, only heavy breathing. You felt sorry for the men trying so hard to perfect their acts. In fact, you felt so sorry that you took on the responsibility for making their jobs easier. You carefully walked by and snatched one of the five skillets from the first man. Putting it in your big basket, you then captured three of the golf balls and one of the bowling pins. All around the room you went until you had a basket full of the jugglers' items.

You noted that the jugglers quickly adjusted to the easing of their burdens—and you also soon noticed that your basket was almost too heavy to carry. Finally you sat down to rest yourself. As you sat there, you began to be aware of some facts.

First, you realized that your basket was too laden to handle. You had gotten more items in it than you had strength to manage. Somehow, you must, because you had no choice, get rid of some of the junk. Second, you could see that, although their burdens were lighter, the jugglers' acts had lost some of their special interest and grace. You had spoiled, just a bit, the art of each man from whom you had stolen a tool. Third, you suddenly saw with uncommon clarity that you had been playing God by judging that these men's lives would be better for your having taken away part of their equipment. Perhaps you were wrong to decide so arbitrarily that the jugglers couldn't maneuver all of their paraphernalia.

So, to make amends for your mistakes, you walked back around the room, returning to each man the thing which you had taken away from him. It was not easy. By then each juggler had gotten used to a simpler trick. He had lost a bit of his skill and was somewhat put out at having to suddenly take his original item and put it back in the show. He would never have noticed if you had not relieved him of it in the first place. Now he is angry. You will have to endure the anger, however, else you will faint under the weight of the basket.

All of our lives are in the hands of a loving and all-knowing Father. The items that we need to learn to juggle in the perfect act for which we were designed are just the right kind and number for our particular skills. Nobody has a right to overrule God and take them away from us. Each person must learn to deal with his own set of problems in his own way. If these are taken away from him, then he will never develop the artistry of his planned performance. He has been given the freedom to lay them down if he chooses—to neglect his act and his place in the larger show. But nobody else has been given the right to do that for him.

* * * * *

After the picture was given to us, we sat in awed silence, letting the magnitude of that growing-up experience sink in. Whose problem is which? I have asked that question of many people. It is difficult to realize that, however much one person loves another, one cannot take on that person's problems. If my friend's husband couldn't handle the whole wife that had just been returned to him, then he would have to learn to do so. She couldn't hide the many facets of herself in the center of an overloaded basket in order to judgmentally "protect him" from his responses to her. Not only would he end up cheated, but she would eventually end up so overburdened that she could no longer function.

As we talked, I realized that I had, along with her, been less than a submissive wife—by our new definition—and had kept many facets of my own life hidden away for many years. We were sad together for a penitent moment and then we began to pray.

"Lord Jesus," we asked, "go back into this life and find the beginning of this need to take the responsibility for someone else's feelings. Please touch the very beginning of the hurt which caused my friend to become so trapped in her prison." As we prayed, we began to see farther and farther back into the life of the little girl. She was a child who had felt responsible, even before she had a concrete memory of it, for the emotional needs of her parents. As she grew older, she took on brothers and sisters, neighbors, friends. It seemed to her that it was her responsibility to take care of the feelings of other people. A terrible burden weighed on her shoulders and her naturally sunny disposition was clouded by the darkness of it.

Jesus, who is the same yesterday, today and tomorrow, was invited to go to the deep hurting source of that need—which began almost in the womb—and heal it; to come down through her life, year by year, freeing her of the compulsion to be the savior of the people in her life. It was, it seemed as we prayed, this need that had made her catch onto the "wifely submission" doctrine in the way she had. But also the need to lay down her basket and have a life of her own had made her slip away occasionally to do something entirely alien. The subsequent guilt which she laid on herself made the already weighty burden almost unmanageable. "Help, dear Lord," we prayed, and He did. Bit by bit we felt the heaviness leaving. We felt His warm joy and the nearness of His loving presence touching that little girl from conception to the present with His healing hands. We saw our now-familiar wastebasket being filled with old hang-ups and preconceived ideas that were not based on love at all but on fear. "Perfect love casts out fear." Whose perfect love? Not ours—His.

As I sat contemplating all the things the Lord had given my lovely friend in the way of insights, I kept seeing the wastebasket waiting, it seemed, for something more. I concentrated my imagination on it and the article that I saw being dropped in was, of all things, a wide, smooth, shiny yellow ribbon. Puzzled, I watched as it slithered into the basket and disappeared. What, Lord, are You showing me now? I like wide yellow ribbon. It is not my idea to have to discard it.

Then I became aware that I share a common piece of misinformation with a lot of Christian wives. We think that to be submissive to our husbands means never to rock the boat—to keep everything as smooth and unruffled as the ribbon in the wastebasket. And, as I looked, I realized that I have always been too insecure to chance disturbing the smooth flowing of life with my husband. I have, because of insecurity, latched onto the "submissive wife" doctrine, just as my friend did. We use our own feelings to justify our behavior and we are calling it Christian living. But is it? Lord, I need You to show me the truth You have in mind for my freedom and for the freedom of not only wives but husbands who are in bondage to the dictates of their own hang-ups. Jesus wants us to discard the blocks and obstructions that keep us from accepting any part of ourselves in order that we may give those selves willingly to Him.

I began to see a picture of a garden. It was smooth and lush, with many good things growing in it. But as I looked, I saw, along with the finished garden, the work of preparation that went into producing it. I saw first the removal of weeds. Then I watched the spading up of the earth—deep shovelfuls of dirt being brought up, turned over, and pounded to pieces. Finally I saw a rake being moved back and forth over the spaded soil to further break and soften it. Before the seeds could be planted, there was a lot of digging and pulverizing and leveling to be done. If the gardener had only smoothed the surface of his plot, he would not have had much of a garden. The soil underneath would have been too hard and firm for the seeds to have taken root. Again I watched the smooth ribbon coiling itself into the waiting wastebasket. I see, Lord.

Being married and living together is a mutual growing. Neither partner can grow if the other is standing still. One's wholeness contributes to the other's and one person's hang-ups contribute to the mate's. When two people accept marriage, they have promised to help each other to deepen and grow, to learn, to change. What is loving behavior in marriage? It is certainly not keeping personality stifled in an effort to act a part. Yet we who deliberately try to live out our old ideas of "submission" are often doing no more than that. I myself have been that way. I have hidden behind doctrines and ideals and have spent a great deal of my time acting like a good Christian wife because I didn't have the courage to get off my smooth ribbon and rock the boat.

I took my deliberations to the team and we spent some time praying for the situation, common to many Christians who really love the Lord and want to do His will. "What is loving behavior?" we asked the Lord. We began to see some new insights.

Supposing one is playing a very difficult role in a play that runs week after week. He steeps himself in the character he is portraying. He makes every move fit into the role and studies to be, inside himself, the person he has chosen to portray. If he is successful, he is a very convincing actor. People who meet him tend to think of him as the character in the play and even treat him as such. I had a young college friend who was Death in the play "Death Takes a Holiday." He worked so hard at it that he lost weight, changed his speech, and developed into a frighteningly realistic Death. For months afterward, he said, his friends treated him slightly differently than before. But Jim was not Death. He was Jim. No matter how well he acted the part, he had to revert finally to the person that he really was. And so it must be in any relationship. We can play and act and be ever so convincing for a while. But eventually the real person will have to come out and be heard from. Husbands and wives can play roles on the surface in the drama of life for years and years. But somewhere or other they will break with the performance.

Is playing a role what God wants us to do in the name of Christian living? I doubt it. Jesus was not a playactor. He was real in every situation. He did say, "Blessed are the peacemakers," but He did not set out to make peace-at-any-price. Peace of spirit was the result of living the kind of life that He lived—open and honest; all of the parts of himself turned willingly to God. Love in this instance was His participation in openness to all of the situations in the life where He found himself. Love was not withholding responses and hiding parts of himself, nor was it performing for the benefit of somebody else. When husbands and wives live the way Jesus did, they do not play out roles in which one or the other hides away a part of himself or herself in order not to upset or displease the other. They trust that God will be in their every move, and then they move—even if it rocks the boat.

Our group came to a lot of individual conclusions about lacks in dealing openly with our mates. I went home to think and ponder what I had learned about the effect of my own insecurities on the growth of my husband. It was not the most encouraging thing I could think of. I was faced with the guilt that a new insight often gives the desperate-to-please child; and I had to give that guilt, along with all of my new knowledge, to the Lord for His light. I set about to do all that as fast as I could (for that is my nature) while I prepared dinner. Before I was well along making a pot of soup, a new Christian neighbor of mine came by for a chat. She is much younger than I, a sweet, intelligent bride who wants more than anything else to do the Lord's will in her life. As we sat visiting, I got up and tossed a handful of raisins into my bubbling soup. She gasped. "You put raisins in your soup?" I nodded, laughing at her surprised expression. "What does your husband think? Mine would be horrified. I'd never dare do such a thing."

I thought of the first time I had put raisins in the soup and of the effect it had had on my family. Yes, it was a shock to my husband. He sputtered and fumed for a moment until he thought about the possibility of tasting the soup. But after he tasted it, he admitted that, although he hadn't originally liked the idea of the raisins, they really tasted pretty good after all.

"Why would you not dare?" I asked my friend, seeing again the wide yellow ribbon slipping out of sight into the wastebasket. "What sort of terrible thing would your Christian husband do to you if he found a raisin in his soup?"

She sputtered sheepishly and we both laughed. Still, I felt that the Lord had given me a humorous picture of a profound truth. My husband might fuss a bit, but in the end it would be a learning and widening experience for him. Must I never dare to do anything because I fear a conflict? Is that what living as a submissive wife is all about? The presence of Jesus as Lord of our lives frees us to face conflict with faith, with confidence that it is a chance for growth, for breaking out of old patterns, for receiving new insights.

Conflict over who I am as a God-created human being is not destructive. I'm sure God's original plan for marriage was not a relationship where we live stereotypes in order to exist without confrontation. Yet there are many of us who are so programmed to a stereotype that we live only half-existences rather than allow any newness to enter—especially lest the newness be born in pain. Looking at the ribbon in the basket, I know I am seeing my old fear of confrontation—a deterrent to the growth and maturity of both my husband and myself. He has suffered from my withholding of my wholeness in order not to upset the status-quo. Perhaps I am alone in that condition, but I have a feeling that I am not. My young friend now jokes about each new encounter as "going home and putting a raisin in Bill's soup." But the experience has shown her, already, that he soon learns to tolerate and sometimes even relish new facets of her creativity. She is finding out that certain conflicts can break the hard ground of the past and ready the soil for new seed which, once planted, grows by the grace of God.

Scripture

"God speaks first in one way, and then in another, but no one notices" (Job 33:14).

"And from pride preserve your servant, never let it dominate me" (Ps. 19:13).

" ' . . . do not worry about how to defend yourselves or what to say, because when the time comes, the Holy Spirit will teach you what you must say' " (Luke 12:12).

"One night the Lord spoke to Paul in a vision, 'Do not be afraid to speak out, nor allow yourself to be silenced. I am with you . . .' I did the planting, Apollos did the watering, but God made things grow" (1 Cor. 3:6).

Chapter 6

Who Is Sitting at My Table?

How do I arrive at priorities in my Christian life?

I was so tired one day that I couldn't manage my
usual work. I had to stop and take stock of the demands I
was making on myself—take a look at my priorities and
my limits. I love people. I am involved with them a great
deal of the time. But it was not always that way. A lonely
"only," I spent many hours of my early life by myself. In
a way, I hid myself away. My mother was almost forty
when I was born and she desperately wanted a baby of
her very own. (She was the oldest in a large family and
no doubt felt obligated, since they were always poor, to
share whatever she had. She told me once that when I
was born she was overjoyed because at last she had a
possession all her own.) Because I was so carefully
watched and supervised, I had a great need to find my
identity. But I knew of no way to achieve it. Many children would have rebelled at an early age. I didn't. In-

stead I suffered from a great deal of undefined, unexpressed anger. When I was finally led to ask the Lord to begin the job of bringing me out of that life of solitary fury, I began to experience many things, some of which I had almost no understanding.

Because I like ideas and puzzles that fit and have no missing pieces, the Lord started handing me, a music teacher to begin with, volumes and volumes of psychology and psychiatry to read. Histories and methods and ideas piled into my head so fast that it spun regularly. I absorbed many of the ideas and philosophies and the methods to give understanding to what I was experiencing. It was exciting to first experience, then read about in a psychology book, and finally find in the New Testament some truth that led me to more light, freedom and life. I became less and less fearful and more and more thrilled with the emergence of wholeness and the realization that there was daily something fresh to help me make a new contact with my beloved Saviour. As I grew to know myself a little more, love myself sometimes, and began to be free enough of the burden of myself to relate to other people, I started to enjoy them more. I could feel God's love flowing through me into real-life situations, and I could see other human beings finding the joy of Jesus' saving and healing power. I knew now that all of my lonely pretend-talk to made-up friends was practice for talking to real live people. I began to realize that my lively make-believe world was holy preparation for something that has happened to me with increasing frequency: I see pictures; I give my imagination to the Lord and then let Him fill it with His special brand of truth. The truth often comes as clear and graphic scenes which tell me more clearly than words can ever do what He wants me (and often my friends) to know.

As I stopped my work this particular morning and rested before the fireplace, I began to see a picture which has been a source of strength and peace for me many times since. The picture began with a banquet hall. The host in this beautiful room was a fine, gracious man, smiling and handsome. As I came in the door, he greeted me warmly. I told him that I had come to work and that I had special gifts for serving food and waiting tables. Would he put me right to work? As he stood thinking, I watched the efforts of the other people working among the banquet tables. I could hardly wait to get started, for I saw a great deal of ineptness among the help.

Instead of assigning me to a job for which I felt well qualified, however, the host led me to a single table set for fourteen people. He pointed to one leg which was about two inches shorter than the others. He lifted the corner of the table to the exact height of the rest and indicated that my job was to stand and hold that corner while the guests sitting there ate their dinner. I was crushed. As I looked around, I could see many jobs which seemed a lot more necessary than the one I was doing. For a long time I fumed at the whole arrangement. Finally, though, I looked around at the people sitting at my table. As I did so, I discovered that the surface of the table was not hard as tables usually are; instead it was flexible. When the man at the corner cut his meat, the table sprung ever so slightly and caused the man sitting next to him to spill his water. Only if I pushed up on the corner to match the pressure of the meat-cutting did everyone eat comfortably. The job took a great deal of concentration. I became so engrossed in it, in fact, that I had no more time to see other things that needed doing or to wish to be doing them.

As I looked at this picture, I began to understand what the Lord was telling me. I had been feeling guilty about not visiting and working my share at the nursing home. I had been remorseful that I had dropped out of a church fellowship group; and there were several people who had asked me for my listening ear and advice to whom I had not been able to respond. I was sorry that I had not written some long-overdue letters, nor had I had time to comfort a woman whose grief had truly touched my heart.

Continuing to explore the meaning of my picture, I began to see that it was He, my Lord, who had brought certain people into my life. And it was my job to do for these specific individuals what needed to be done. As I counted those with whose lives I did have a real involvement, I found that there were (of course!) exactly fourteen. He was showing me that if I did what He wanted me to do for those fourteen of His children, He would be responsible to care for the rest.

"But what about the fact that they *expect* things of me?" I wailed to Him.

"What *I* expect of you is the matter of importance."

The message became clearer and clearer as I faced honestly my motives for the things I was doing. My friends in the nursing home would look down on me if I neglected to work there. My image in the eyes of someone else would fall below my high standards if I did not do what was expected of me. I would be doing a job in the

Lord's banquet hall not for Him but for my own glory and satisfaction. My leg of the table was supporting fourteen people and that was not only all the Lord wanted me to do; it also was all I had either strength or creativity to accomplish. Therefore it was up to me to yield up my role in my own and my friends' eyes, doing only what *He* had put before me. It is hard to say, in one way or another, to a needy person, "You are not at my table. I care but I have all I can handle without ministering to you." But that was my message. And, surprisingly enough, as I acted on it, I began to feel better, happier, freer—to get more work done in less time and with less tension.

The hardest part, though, was to put my guilt in God's big wastebasket. We have been so programmed to witness by our works that we sometimes become "workaholics." We go harder and faster and never stop to realize that we are not always doing for God what we find ourselves engaged in. Many times our efforts are based on long-ago insecurity about being satisfactory children to hard-to-please parents. Often the more "Christian" the family has been the more pressure the children feel to live out their parents' image. If seeing their children perform as much work as they can possibly turn out is what will make the parents happy, the children will usually do all in their power to oblige. If we can please our parents only with a certain prescribed set of behavior patterns, we feel deep inside that we can please God in only that same limited fashion. God was telling me differently. I began to see that He had created me and it was up to Him to assign my tasks. What a relief! How much more free I was to do my best for the people sitting at my table after I found that I did not have to choose my work, my co-workers, or those whom God had given to somebody else.

Though you might not need a thought-picture as I did, God will, I am sure, show you just as surely and graphically who should be at your table.

Scripture

"Plans multiply in the human heart, but the purpose of Yahweh stands firm" (Prov. 19:21).

"When that time comes I will rescue the lame, and gather the strays, and I will win them praise and renown when I restore their fortunes" (Zeph. 3:19b).

" ' . . . the way you think is not God's way but man's' " (Mark 8:33b).

"People must think of us as Christ's servants, stewards entrusted with the mysteries of God. What is expected of stewards is that each one should be found worthy of his trust. Not that it makes the slightest difference to me whether you, or indeed any human tribunal, find me worthy or not. I will not even pass judgment on myself. True, my conscience does not reproach me at all, but that does not prove that I am acquitted: the Lord alone is my judge" (1 Cor. 4:1-5).

Chapter 7

The Other Room Has a Red Sofa

How can I be sure that my ideas are from God?

My picture of the table to which my Lord had assigned me sustained me and helped me to grow deeply toward inner peace. For several weeks I kept it to myself. But after a while I realized that it was a lesson for all of us. I began to share it; and those with whom I shared it passed it along further. It proved a new source of organization for our Christian community.

Finally, though, I had a critic. He is a man who is well founded in the doctrine of "reality." Although he has finally made a stab at accepting the part of reality which is the most real of all, the spiritual part, he still finds it hard to trust himself where it is involved. When he heard the story of the table, he said, "It sounds like rationalization to me. I wouldn't trust my imagination like that. If I started imagining things, how would I know it wasn't just *me*? How can I feel sure my ideas are from the Lord—especially when they fit so well with what I'd like to do or think myself?''

I could hear what he was saying very well. I have lived much of my life in contact with people who have the unspoken premise that if something is pleasant or satisfying or, most especially, fun, it couldn't be from God. Nonsense and fantasy are an equal waste in the minds of those people.

"Don't be foolish . . . that's just your imagination . . ." sounds in my ears from many of the grown-ups in my childhood. "God's directives are all in the Bible. You mustn't think of anything that isn't there" came across to me, too, loud and clear. I knew how my friend was feeling. Still, I have heard and seen and felt many wonderful and obviously holy things in my inner world, the fruit of which have proven again and again that they were from God. I was just beginning to trust my imagination. I was learning also to trust the personal relationship with a Person there who ministered to me in ways that had, for all to see, improved my life's joy and effectiveness. Where is the key, I asked the Spirit, to free my friend from the bondage of failing to trust a part of himself that is as much a function and member as his hands and feet? How did I learn to trust my own inner pictures?

When I was alone as a child, I lived much of my time in my imagination. It was comfortable country for me. Learning about the Lord Jesus and finally meeting Him personally was a process that automatically included my imagination. As soon as I met Him, I gave it to Him just as I did the rest of me. I asked Him to use it for His glory because, as soon as I became acquainted with Him, I saw that I had always before used it for *my* glory. Still, practicing imagining for my own esteem made it possible for me to see a greater and purer holiness as soon as *He* walked into my imagination. All this was my experience; the friend in front of me had never had that experience. He had always lived in the "world of reality" which scorned anything which he classed as "unreal." My definition of reality included the solid fact of my vivid imagination. His did not. How, then, could I relate to him from a perspective so opposite?

Well, alone I could not relate to him at all. Without the Spirit to sustain me, I respond to all criticism by literally dissolving. I have no self-confidence on my own. But with Jesus all things really are possible. So I turned my voice over to the Holy Wisdom and waited to hear what kind of liaison He would provide between the two worlds.

* * * * *

Supposing you owned a house—a big house with upstairs, downstairs and basement. After you met the Lord, you told Him that the house now belonged to Him—that He was free to go into every part of it. You took Him at once to the light, bright upstairs—the place of the spirit. There the two of you had a great time. Then you got up the courage to take Him to the basement where your old subconscious secrets lay in darkness. Sure enough, as you explored the dark basement, He shone His light and you began to know and understand the dusty contents there. You took Him into your work room, your special place of creativity and construction, and asked Him to help you with your projects. You took Him to your office where He graciously assisted you with the bills and financial puzzles of your life. You took Him

to the kitchen where you ate and drank into the every-
dayness of your life.

But supposing there was a room in the back of the
house that you seldom used. It had a lock on it so you
rarely opened it. He indicated that He might like to
spend a little time there. Pleased, you took Him in and
showed it to Him. You realized that it had a scant
amount of furniture, that He might be more comfortable
if there were more. So you offered Him the key, telling
Him that nobody else had a key and the room was all His
to do with as He wished. He thanked you and took the
key.

When you returned from work that evening, you went
up and knocked on the door to see what your Lord had
done to the room. You were astonished. He had rear-
ranged the small amount of used furniture and put in
some new things you'd never seen before: a red sofa, a
picture, an end table, a rug. The room looked beautiful,
rich and warm. "Could this be *my* old room?" you asked
in astonishment. "I gave Him this place and look what
He has done to it. I love it!"

Knowing that you had given the Lord the only key
and permission, as well, to do whatever He liked to the
room, it would be most unlikely that you would doubt
that it was indeed He who had refurnished the room—
especially if it was beautiful and you liked it. If you
thought it was ugly, you might feel differently. But
beauty, warmth, light, creativity, constructiveness are
part of any situation that has been exposed to the Lord.

In our culture, founded as so much of it is on logic
and reality, the everyday value of the imagination is re-
served for a few artists and mostly ignored by the rest of

us. It is a small, rarely used room in our lives, furnished with a bit of old, drab furniture left over from childhood. But it is a part of each one of us—a part which God has given us. He created the mind just as it is. Listening to small children playing, we soon realize that the human mind is full of richness and beauty, particularly in the area of the imagination. When I gave my imagination to the Lord and He took it, He began to fix up the furniture to suit himself. Nobody else has the key. It is no longer "my" room. It is His room. Therefore, whatever things I see there, I have to trust to His responsibility.

It was my choice in the first place to ask Jesus into my life. I asked Him to illuminate my subconscious, to bring life to my spirit, to light my mind, to stir my creativity. I asked Him to furnish my imagination with whatever He needed to cause it to glorify Him. Can I not trust Him to do that? If I am trusting Him, then I must also trust the new furniture He has placed in this small room of my house.

*   *   *   *   *

It took my critic a while to come to terms with this new concept, just as it had taken me a while to begin to put my whole trust in the total Lordship of Jesus. But as we did, new dimensions began to be evident. As I prayed with people for inner healing, I noticed that I was often given the gift of a clear mental picture of a baby or small child in a situation which was painful or full of fear. As I began to trust these pictures and pray them through, I saw that it was the Lord Jesus' new furniture in my imagination—for the glory of God in the wholeness of those He loved.

Sometimes the pictures were funny. I was praying for a gray-haired lady once who seemed overcome with fears. We had prayed far back in her life, asking for Jesus to heal hurt after hurt. We thought we had finished and were sitting in silence, absorbing His beautiful presence when I suddenly "saw" a little tiny girl in overalls running as fast as she could, brown pigtails streaming out behind her and terror on her face. Behind her was a large dog. My own body tensed as I experienced her fear, helplessness, her breath tight in her throat. Without thinking, I began to call upon Jesus:

"Lord, touch that child, please. Take her to safety in Your arms; take the terror out of her heart as she runs from the dog. Touch the dog and turn his growls into friendly sounds. Please, dear Lord, heal that frightening experience in the little girl's subconscious."

By the time I finished, the lady was quietly weeping. I knew that her tears were melting an old, old terror, so I sat in silence. After a while, through her sniffles, she began to laugh.

"I was so busy reliving my old forgotten experience that I almost forgot to correct your mistake. That wasn't a dog. It was a coyote." A mistake in my picture? Yes, I saw into the lady's hurting subconscious by the power of the Spirit, but I didn't recognize the creature of her terror. It was not *my* room but the Lord's. It was He who knew what to show and then heal to make His child not only done with that particular hurt from the past, but strong in her tenderness toward other people's fear.

Scripture

"The word of Yahweh was addressed to me as follows, 'Son of man, what do you mean by this proverb common throughout the land of Israel: Days go by and visions fade?

'Very well, tell them, "The Lord Yahweh says this: I will put an end to this proverb; it shall never be heard in Israel again." From now on there will be no empty vision, no deceitful prophecy in the House of Israel, since it is I, Yahweh, who will speak . . ." ' (Ezek. 12:21-25).

"I will stand on my watchtower, and take up my post on my battlements, watching to see what he will say to me, what answer he will make to my complaints. Then Yahweh answered and said. 'Write the vision down, inscribe it on tablets to be easily read, since this vision is for its own time only; eager for its own fulfillment, it does not deceive; if it comes slowly, wait, for come it will, without fail. See how he flags, he whose soul is not at rights, but the upright man will live by his faithfulness' " (Hab 2:1-5).

" . . . and when they did not find the body, they came back to tell us they had seen a vision of angels who declared he was alive" (Luke 24:23).

" . . . and the grace that he gave me had not been fruitless" (1 Cor 15:10).

"And for anyone who is in Christ, there is a new creation; the old creation has gone, and now the new one is here. It is all God's work" (2 Cor. 5:17).

"As his fellow workers, we beg you once again not to neglect the grace of God that you have received" (2 Cor 6:1).

"I will move on to the visions and revelations I have had from the Lord" (2 Cor. 12:1).

"The nearer you go to God, the nearer he will come to you" (James 4:8).

Chapter 8

Beads on a String

Is prayer ever wasted?

Once a number of years ago a friend came to me because she had a problem. This was during the time I was still moving up the steep mountain toward a personal confrontation with the living Christ, so I didn't know Him yet. But I believed in Him and I believed in prayer. I don't know how much I really believed in *answered* prayer. Nevertheless, I prayed regularly and diligently.

The lady's problem was that she had a very seriously ill child for whom the doctors held out little hope. She and her husband were calling themselves atheists. She couldn't bring herself to actually ask me to pray for her child; but she wanted help from a power more than herself, which somehow she connected with me. Of course I did pray for the baby, as intensely as I knew how. As I did so, somewhere deep inside, I knew an absolute conviction that the child would recover. At that point was born in me an intense love for the little boy and more especially for his mother. I began to pray regularly for her, asking God that she be free of the bondage of her professed non-whatever, and become a believer.

Some time later I took a step from a purely intellectual belief in Jesus as Lord to a meeting of Him in a personal encounter. His gift to me, based not at all on my worthiness, was the gift of spiritual life. I had such a longing inside me not only to know *about* but to really *experience* that love that I saw hinted at in my small experiences with believing. This new dimension intensified all of my prayers for everyone I loved, my atheist friend included. And by then I realized that she could not really be an unbeliever. (I have serious doubts that anyone is, deep inside. God made us with a need for Him and we can never explain it away.) She was, instead, an insecure person afraid of offending her husband. He was a good, kind man. But he was convinced that all religion was weakness and that his own efforts at good living were entirely sufficient. His scorn was impenetrable.

I know all too well the sacrifice involved, at first glance, in making an independent turn and giving one's life to Jesus after having teamed up with an unbelieving mate. It is especially frightening if the relationship has a good deal of dependency in it. I know a number of people who long to make a commitment to Jesus but are afraid of the gap they feel it might cause in their relationship with spouses. I guess this is even more true when the spouses are adamant about "religious fanatics," "the foolish unreality of faith," "unrealistic expectations from the magic of prayer," "religion as a cop-out for weak people," "biblical prophecy is hogwash," and other such often-heard comments. I am quite convinced that most such statements are in reality spiritual "teenage rebellion" about which God is much more understanding and patient than I am. When a person has counted the cost, evaluated the risk, and then gone ahead with the leap-of-faith, spouse notwithstanding, it is hard to be patient with the ones who haven't done it yet. It is so good to have the sure awareness of the loving hand of our Saviour constantly in control of one's life that I, at least, fairly dance with impatience for those I love. In any case, I prayed harder than ever for my friend and her little son. Nothing whatever seemed to be happening. The child grew and grew, a special boy with a depth of awareness that most children don't show. I continued, with sighs of resignation, to keep my friend on my prayer list. My Father must have laughed at my grumblings.

Finally one day as I was cleaning a closet, I really let go and told God how I felt. I told Him I had been praying for this lady as long as I was going to. I was through! If He wasn't planning to answer that particular prayer, then I intended to use my prayer energy on something else—so there, God!

And then I saw the loveliest picture. It was as if a long string of beads had been tossed at random, with a loose thread through all their centers, only barely holding them from scattering to the far corners. The beads were many colors, several sizes, but each of a crevassed material like the meat of a ripe watermelon. The sunshine sparkled from them into every part of the room. I gasped in delight. What, Lord? What are they?

Into my mind came the words, clear as a voice: "No prayer is ever wasted." I sat for long moments, debating the meaning of my image. The string through the center? As I pondered, the beads came into focus again. This time it was as if someone had pulled the two ends of the thread and suddenly the whole collection of beads had lined themselves up on their glowing string. I saw what He was telling me.

I don't have God's eternal timetable in mind. Since there are millions of people in the world and we have no idea what influence we have on the lives of each other, the logistics of answering prayer for the ultimate good of all entirely escapes us. We pray for right-now answers. But His love is what motivates the prayer. It runs through our prayer requests as a consistent thread, connecting us with the will of the Father who is love in person. A prayer never falls unnoticed at the side of the road of life. When all of the things in God's timetable have come about, then He pulls the thread and lines up every random prayer, made at odd times and in differing moods but still made in love. "No prayer is ever wasted" has become a source of great joy for me. It relieves me of the worry that this particular lady or anyone else will fail to know the good that I pray for them, or that my time and concern in praying has been lost.

Besides the discarding of my worries about whether or not my friend will eventually come to the Lord, I see, too, that I am being asked to discard my old concepts of "good." Sometimes it looks to me as if good is best served by one thing and sometimes another. Only God himself knows what is meant by *truly good* for everyone who loves Him—let alone for everyone in the world. His timing of all the events in all of our lives is totally mind-boggling. For me to decide what is ultimately right is impossible. Perhaps a part of the lesson I learned about the prayers for my friend and her son is that I will never know, nor have to, what is perfectly correct for her—the time and the circumstances and the depth of her own feelings. I know my basic prayer for her, that she will come to know the Saviour, is perfectly in the will of God. But though I do not know the details of God's plan, I am reassured that I am effective in the big scheme of God's glory and beauty even when I don't understand at all where that scheme is going.

Turning to Jesus in the face of a scornful mate takes great courage. Courage is a gift of God. I cannot contrive it, no matter how I try. And I myself am most particularly lacking in it. When confronted with anything from a non-skier's ride on the lift to a sermon before a congregation, I am reduced to jelly and have to depend entirely on the presence of the Holy Spirit for my courage. I know now that nothing in the world is as important or as joyful as turning one's life over to the Holy Trinity. But until it happened to me, I had no way of realizing that this was true. I can be very sympathetic, if I look at it that way, with those who fear any new step—especially one so great as the leap of faith which gives one's whole self away, even to the Lord. At last, though, I am finally able to realize that when the longing for Him is strong enough, when one is at the point of desperation, then the gift of courage will be there from God himself. My prayers, founded on the love which ran like a thread through my beads, will continue to activate that longing in another person. I don't know exactly how it happens. I just know that even a little bit of love is magnetic, drawing and pulling toward the source of love—God. As the time draws near, my prayers for my friend will begin to line themselves up in accord with God's plan: He wants us all. He longs for us to love Him and turn our lives over to Him willingly. So when all things are right, when that person is sick of sin and selfishness, then my prayers, along with everything else, will draw together and bring another soul into the joy of the Lord.

Scripture

" . . . they called to you for help and they were saved, they never trusted you in vain" (Ps. 22:5).

"Yahweh looks down from heaven, he sees the whole human race; from where he sits he watches all who live on the earth, he who molds every heart takes note of all men do" (Ps. 33:13-16).

"Long before they call I shall answer; before they stop speaking I shall have heard" (Isa. 65:24).

"And if you have faith, everything you ask for in prayer you will receive" (Matt. 21:22).

"No one can come to me unless he is drawn by the Father who sent me and I will raise him up on the last day" (John 6:44).

"But when Christ is revealed—and he is your life— you too will be revealed in all your glory with him" (Col. 3:4).

"The Lamb came forward to take the scroll from the right hand of the One sitting on the throne, and when he took it, the four animals prostrated themselves before him and with them the twenty-four elders; each one of them was holding a harp and had a golden bowl full of incense made of the prayers of the saints" (Rev. 5:8).

Chapter 9

The Golden Statue

How can a God of love also be a God of wrath?

"If you want a lot of heat without much light, then start people talking about religion," my grandmother used to say. I often wondered what she meant. Of all the sources of joy and peace between people, it appeared to me, religion ought to be the best. Instead it often seems to be a trigger for the most brutal kinds of disagreement. I think I have finally figured out the reason. Everyone wants more intensely than anything else in his life to know love, to have access to its source. We don't just passively desire it either. We *must* have it to survive as humans; and inside ourselves, where it matters, we all know that fact. We try desperately to locate the love which we require; and because we have been led to believe that we can find it in "religion," that is where we look. We expect a sure-fire source.

But frequently we don't find the satisfaction of our

longing in religion at all. Religion, per se, is no guarantee of love. A particular group of people may have a unity of sorts—perhaps the unity of being different from others or of being possessed by a goal or purpose. However, if their religion does not point to the source of love—Father, Son and Spirit—then whatever else it does do will be second rate and less than satisfying. Whatever one's life is focused upon with the greatest degree of intensity it is his "religion," be it witchcraft, Jesus Christ, or anything in between. If he is in it with the unrecognized hope of filling the need for love which God himself has built into his inner self, a man will defend his religion with a passion. It is quite obvious to me that much heart and almost no light at all is generated by defensiveness. When I catch myself being defensive, I try to get to the bottom of it as fast as I can and ask the Lord to heal it.

That is why it upsets me no end when people describe me as "religious." There is a vast difference between being religious and knowing and loving a living Lord. He makes life vibrant and full of surprises; He makes me compassionate, flexible. People who are religious quite often come across as stuffy. I don't want to be like that. I want to be part of a larger and larger group who happily discuss their Lord Jesus and the wonder of His presence which generates not heat-without-light but more and more gracious love for one another. Jesus did say that they shall know we are His disciples by the love we have *one for another.*

One day I was supposed to address a local seminar. I like to speak to most groups, but the Lord knows me even better than I know myself. He knows how much I need to have a nicely typed, prepared speech in my hands. Even when He changes my talk from one end to the other after I have begun, He always gives me something secure to hold on to when I start. Sometimes I receive the idea in the middle of the night and it is a week before I get around to writing it down. Other times I sit down at the typewriter and there it is, complete without alteration. As soon as I have a talk in mind, I know that within a few hours I will be invited to make one. This circumstance was no exception. I received the idea while I washed the breakfast dishes and before my hands were dry, the phone rang with an invitation to be part of a seminar made up of, to quote the chairperson, "all sorts of mostly Christians."

"What approach do you think you could have for an assembly like that?" she asked timidly. I laughed to myself. The Holy Spirit had been giving me a dissertation on love, "which will certainly be of common interest to them all," I assured her. I felt, although she said nothing, that she was less than satisfied with a subject so ordinary. So I began to pray that my talk would not just be *about* love, but would be so filled with it that my audience would catch a glimpse of the presence of Him who is love itself. One of the reasons I enjoy speaking is that since I have never been trained and have no faith in myself at all, my only choice, under those circumstances, is to turn myself over to the Spirit and let Him do it for me. What He does is always such a breathtaking surprise to me that I fairly burst with happiness.

Papers in hand and prayers in my heart, I approached the seminar only to find most of the participants still eating their lunch. I sat listening to their conversation, much of which was about the weather and sports, recipes and their children. But one little group was noticeably intense and angry. Of course, I might have guessed it—they were discussing religion.

"I just won't read the Old Testament," one man was saying. "It is nothing but bloodshed. The thing is so full of killing that it makes me sick. God is supposed to be loving and yet He let all sorts of ugliness happen just because some of the people weren't on the side of those arrogant Old Testament Jews. Why should it have mattered if they worshipped Baal as long as they were really worshipping? Judgment and wrath and all that stuff is just not what I want to hear about." The rest of the group continued in the same vein for a bit. Then a new topic emerged, the best-selling book *Life After Life*.

"I don't think it's any good at all!" A woman's voice was hot with emotion. "If we believed what that book says, there's no judgment. We can just do whatever we want. The Bible promises judgment, and I believe in it." Her stern face showed concern that whoever was judged to have punishment coming to him would surely not be cheated out of it. This comment and the ones that followed it sounded to me like a quite opposite point of view—longing, maybe—from the one expressed by the first man.

My hands began to shake. "Lord," I prayed in panic, "are you sure that these people will be able to hear any of my words about love? Hadn't I better talk about something else?" As I prayed, a great peace filled me. "Love is the strongest force in the world," He seemed to be saying to me. "Go ahead and talk about it." I walked to the front of the room, trembling with every step. My prepared talk? I didn't know. When I opened my mouth, it was entirely possible that I would talk about love in a way new even to me.

*   *   *   *   *

Imagine with me a statue bigger than life and made out of what appears to be pure gold. It stands tall and beautiful in the sunshine. Then imagine that a light a thousand times brighter than the sun begins to shine on it. We'll call that light love—pure love. It is not the emotionalism nor the sentiment we have come to think of as love but is, instead, the love that God *is.* As it beams on the statue, it becomes hotter and hotter. Ever more intense as it flows over the gold, it radiates in all directions, filling its surroundings with holy light. The gold of the statue glows. For a moment everything seems suspended in this pure light of love. And then a strange thing happens: part of the statue's face begins to change shape. It sags and slips, and before long it has started to melt and slide down the side of the figure, leaving a gaping hole where the face had been. Presently a part of the shoulder and arm melt, too, and then the back and a leg. The bright light continues to shine, showing clearly the craggy parts of the gold statue that have endured through the melting action of the intense heat. The heat and light have done away with all but the valuable and beautiful metal, cleaning out wax and paint and all counterfeits and less-than-pure substances. The light appears to have decided which is to be eliminated and immediately set about to do the eliminating. The wonderful presence of pure love seems to have destroyed.

If I were the statue, I would feel that I had been judged and that the wrath of God had descended on me when the wax began to melt and run away. If it were my city or my nation that the bright light had come upon, I would feel that they had been judged and the wrath of God had descended on them, too. But if I were the gold, I would joyously feel that whatever was less-than-gold had been removed from me. If the love of God is so intense that it removes, on contact, all which is not love in everyone's life, then it is doing a great good in taking away what is less than perfect. This great good might seem painful and heavy to bear at the time, but in God's overall plan and purpose it all comes out of His nature of love.

Once I asked a large group of people what they thought was the strongest force in existence. Their answers included earthquakes, hurricanes, hydrogen bombs, machinery of various kinds. Nobody seemed to remember that these are all forces of destruction. They are powers that tear down. What power goes in where destruction has been and begins to rebuild? It's the power of love, people for people as well as individual for individual. When God created the earth and everything in it and then put mankind on it, He was doing an act of love. When God put a special mark on Cain to protect him from death, His was an act of love. But let's back up a bit and take another look at Cain. When God judged Cain's murder of his brother, *He was doing an act of love.* Remember our parents saying to us, "This spanking hurts me more than it does you. I *have* to spank you because I love you"? God loves people so much that He cannot leave them to go their own sinful way. Out of His righteousness, justice, goodness and, yes, *love,* He must judge sin.

In any case, my search through the Holy Scriptures gave me a new understanding of God's caring for us. Da-

vid saw it much more clearly than many of the Old Testament writers. He felt comfortable to "tell it like it was"
to God because he knew for sure the great kindness and
eternal forgiveness that is God.

As I read the words in the Old Testament, I could see
more and more clearly why God needed to send His Son
to earth. He must not only show us what His Father is
like, but he must also re-establish the relationship with
Him that we all long for. In fulfilling this, Jesus gave
himself as the sacrificial lamb and brought us back into
the freedom of knowing God's love by taking on himself
sin's punishment—death.

Of course we know that even after Jesus came and
showed us the nature of God in person, there were many
who did not see. They still insisted upon trying to win
and keep His love with man-made rules. Nothing is
harder for us to accept than God's grace—His love to us
when we are not lovable.

Children die without love. Civilizations perish. The
results of cultures crumble unless the creative force of
love lives in them. Whatever is not of this force is like the
wax in our little "suppose" at the beginning. Less than
pure gold disappears when white hot light is beamed
against it. What *seems* to be the wrath of God is His pure
love, melting away everything of sin, self and death. Our
lives can be of a positive, creative nature. We have the
choice in our hands: the choice of love or less-than-love;
the choice of God or other gods; of Christ or false mes-
siahs; of self or Saviour.

* * * * *

It seemed to me that my talk was finished with a
flourish. It had been a bit different from my original
plan, but not much. My confidence had reached a new

high. But then the questions began. (How can a person answer questions about God? All I can ever do is tell what I have learned from the Scripture. The minute someone asks me a question, I begin to panic. Experience God? Yes, yes, yes. But explain Him? Explain prayer? No, not I.) So I was not self-confident at all when the queries began, especially from older more resolute people. Because I didn't have the answers, I had to open my mouth and let the Lord speak. It was His idea to put me in the seminar, so I decided it was up to Him to speak if anything was to be said.

"How can you fit that theory," my first questioner demanded, "with references to hell and damnation?" The man who spoke had a good Bible background. I knew, myself, that there are many references in Jesus' teachings to "eternal damnation." How, indeed? So, Holy Spirit, please hear my favorite prayer again: *help!*

* * * * *

Jesus spent much of His time telling and, more important, showing us the loving and forgiving nature of God. The picture which He gave us was of a Father so anxious to find each of His children that He would spare no effort to reach anyone. Someone explained once that it is as if God were a man in a boat so determined to come ashore that he would go around and around an inaccessible island trying to find even the smallest spot to land. No matter how seemingly unworthy, Jesus showed us that each man is of value. Therefore, we've all asked, how could this same loving Father condemn anyone to everlasting punishment with no chance of reprieve?

Let's consider the word "damnation" or "condemnation." If you lay down beside the railroad track, went to sleep and while sleeping threw your arm on the rail and had it amputated by the train, your brother might say, "Oh dear, you are condemned to a life of one-armed-ness." Yet in so saying, your brother would not himself be condemning you. Neither would he be saying that God—or anybody else—had condemned you. He would merely be stating the unfortunate fact that one-armed-ness was a result of what you had done. Jesus' words telling us, or the scribes and Pharisees about "eternal damnation" were not so much a threat of punishment to be meted out as statements about the results of certain behavior, the results of human choices. God is not an unforgiving ogre who delights in sending souls forever into darkness. Hell is the horrible state of being totally turned away from God.

By telling us about this turned-away condition and how horrible it is, Jesus was emphasizing that if we live in certain ways and do or fail to do certain things, we have *condemned ourselves* to the away-from-God darkness by the way we have lived. God himself did not condemn us. Instead, we chose the path, maybe not once but again and again. It is easy to imagine the sadness with which Jesus described to His followers the state they would be in if they failed to turn and stay turned toward God.

The Word of God is clear that the choice to follow Him must be made during this period we call life. We do not know how that works out in every little detail for every individual. But we can fully trust this God of love to give every individual who has ever lived the opportunity to make a clear choice.

I feel that one of the most important discards in our

lives is the idea that God is lying in wait for us to make a mistake so that He can punish us. As I pray for people's inner healing, it is amazing to me how many of them have, deep below the threshold of intellect, this idea of God. A good assignment to help in sensing the consistency between the love and the justice of God is to read the First Letter of John in as many translations as possible. John, himself old and ready to go to his Lord, listened to the Holy Spirit with his pen poised, and the flow of his words gives me confidence in the accuracy of his recording. God does not have two faces, one of mercy and one of judgment. All His attributes come from one course: *God is love.*

Scripture

"God does not see as man sees; man looks at appearances but Yahweh looks at the heart" (1 Sam. 16:7).

"He dug a pit, hollowed it out, only to fall into his own trap! His spite recoils on his own head, his brutality falls back on his own skull" (Ps. 7:15-16).

"But I for my part rely on your love, Yahweh; let my heart rejoice in your saving help. Let me sing to Yahweh for the goodness he has shown me" (Ps. 13:5).

"I am listening. What is Yahweh saying? What God is saying means peace for his people, for his friends, if only they renounce their folly; for those who fear him, his saving help is near . . ." (Ps. 85:8-9).

"Your own wickedness is punishing you, your own apostasies are rebuking you . . ." (Jer. 2:19).

"Those who serve worthless idols forfeit the grace that was theirs" (John 2:9).

" 'I tell you most solemnly, whoever keeps my word will never see death' " (John 8:51).

" 'As the Father has loved me, so I have loved you. Remain in my love. If you keep my commandments you will remain in my love, just as I have kept my Father's commandments and remain in his love . . . This is my commandment: love one another as I have loved you' " (John 15:9, 10, 12).

"Christ redeemed us from the curse of the Law by being cursed for our sake" (Gal. 3:13).

" . . . if anyone lets himself be dominated by anything, he is a slave to it" (2 Pet. 2:19b).

"Every branch in me that bears no fruit he cuts away, and every branch that does bear fruit he prunes to make it bear even more . . . As the Father has loved me, so I have loved you" (John 15:2, 9).

Chapter 10

Follow the Yellow Brick Road

How can I get out of depression?

"Follow the yellow brick road...." I suppose I'll hopelessly date myself if I tell how much I loved Judy Garland's rendition of that song in *The Wizard of Oz*. It did things to my insides, not in the least related to the plot of the story. Later, when I heard the song based on the scripture, "Seek ye first the kingdom of God," I felt again the old bubbling joy of the yellow brick road. (Never mind that Judy's road was wide and handsome, and scripture says the path to the Kingdom is narrow. They still have a similar kind of call for me.) And besides, there is something inside of me that tells me whether I am on or off that highway. Sometimes I have gotten off for a while and don't hear it. But finally, every time, the still small voice of the Spirit brings me back again.

There are plenty of interesting and inviting side

roads, though. I have tried several of them. My child-hood isolation and lack of freedom made me so miserable that I didn't dare face the pain. For some time I played the game of being the person I wanted to be and wouldn't allow myself to look at any feelings to the contrary. It was hard work. Keeping strong emotions out of con-sciousness is a thoroughly demanding activity. So when-ever I became too tired from the strain of not looking at my own inner world, I stepped off the yellow brick road onto a little path called "Doing Things." It was winding and inviting and full of surprises; and it did a fairly ef-fective job of keeping me comfortable. In short, I made myself busy. I went so fast and did so much that I didn't see that I was going in a direction quite apart from seek-ing God's Kingdom. Even though I usually kept busy with church functions, it was really Phoebe's kingdom that I was looking for: affirmation and success, approval (particularly my own). God did not desert me, though. His Kingdom was there—just out of sight on the other side of my frantic activity.

After a while, I heard a little sound. As I paused to identify it, I recognized my homecoming refrain; and I stopped where I was and hunted my way back to the road to the Kingdom. Busyness is a side road that I still find frequently inviting, even though I am now able to con-front my feelings much more readily. I find it inviting be-cause inner perfection hasn't come yet, and I am not fond of my own inadequacies. Pretending to be all things to all people—efficient, able, strong and wise; pretend-ing to be those things by doing as much as I can still tempts me.

Another side road that I have taken and continue to

find intriguing is the one labeled "Deciding." I love to know what is happening—to keep the pieces of my puzzle in order, to figure things out. I often sneak off onto a path where I can use my toy bulldozer to run the road where I please. There are several little variations on this lane, too. I like to manipulate my own life. Instead of giving it over to Him who made me and let Him run it the way He knows is best, I sometimes enjoy arranging my activities and my feelings and my friendships to suit myself. I can push the pieces of my life into all kinds of insidious patterns that look almost like the big one God has for me. But that road leads off into a dead end, just as does the path of manipulating other people. Sometimes I have fallen into that trap, too, especially "in the name of Jesus." If I can arrange circumstances so that someone will acknowledge Him, then I am pleased with myself. "Winning souls for Jesus" can be a self-gratification path, one that is full of pride. Nobody comes to Him, truly, until his inner need for the love of God has prodded him into turning there. I may be a light in that direction, but I can never move someone else. Forgetting that fact is a landmark on a road which is far from the clear light of my yellow brick one.

The worst side road I have ever taken was one I followed for a long, long time. It was parallel to the real way toward the Kingdom almost like a service road which seemed to be going to the same place. I followed it because it promised me safe protection against finding out the truth about myself and dealing constructively with it. And it went along so close to the main thoroughfare that I could almost feel that I was on the right track. I know now that I chose to follow it; it was a great moment in my life when I saw how truly I had chosen to do so and how I could as truly choose again to stop walking along the service road and get back on the Holy Highway. The highway sign on that road was labeled "Depression." It turned ever so slightly from lightness and brightness down a hill into a shaded area where the sunshine was diffused by many tall trees. In this place I was safe from confronting the things buried inside myself which were causing my problems. I could be content with knowing that I felt depressed without having to define the reasons—and, more important, do something about them.

On the surface there were no really logical reasons for me to be depressed. I had a good husband, four healthy, intelligent children, a home in the country which was adequate if not elegant. I went to church and belonged to several groups. I had interesting hobbies. I had skills enough to warrant the praise and admiration of other people. I was in reasonably good health except when my body periodically demanded that I stop and think about the darkness I continued to have inside me. It was not the darkness of a "life of sin." It was just the lack of light that comes with having one's head in a depression in the sand.

Jesus had a hand on my life. I knew it subconsciously even when I had forgotten. His was the map from which had been constructed the road of life; therefore He knew, even if I didn't, that I had wandered off on a side road leading nowhere. I'm sure that's why He began singing to me a little song of enticement that sounded just off to my right. As I listened, I began to wish I could find a way back. As soon as I began to wish for it, it began to appear. Books came along, since He knows how much I like to find new ideas in books. Friends began to emerge who had the ability to show me the necessary affirmation which freed me to look away from the shadows into the light of reality. The Inner Healing team was formed. We began to ask for insights. Finally I saw why I had chosen the road down into depression. It was less painful to be miserable than it was to see how far from wholeness I really was.

I was far from wholeness, and so were my friends. The depth of our inadequacy at the side of what God is over-whelmed me completely. In that condition of abysmal nothingness, I suddenly saw the light. God had created me and redeemed me *in spite of myself.* I am a doer. I have always liked to accomplish. The lowest spot in the valley came when I faced up to my own utter helpless-ness. There I lay, flat on my back in the bottom of an abyss. But above me was the caring love of Jesus offering to raise me up and make me whole. Gingerly I put my hand in His and began to inch into a sitting position. I could choose, still, and I chose in that moment not to al-low myself the cop-out of depression any more. I saw my overwhelming pessimism. I saw my emotional retarda-tion, my fearfulness, my insecurity, my need for the child-affirmation which I had never received. I saw the inadequacy of my mask and my pretense. I saw my fear of criticism. I saw my need to be dominated and my dis-like for that domination. I saw that, in every instance in my life, I had chosen a path, out of several alternatives, and how many of my choices had led me farther into de-pression.

It was an ugly sight. At that point of ugliness, I delib-erately elected to start back to the yellow brick road as fast as I could. Its song suddenly became the loudest call in my life. It was time for me to begin asking the Holy Spirit to permeate my conscious and my subconscious as well, to reveal and to heal. I began to be aware that my hurts and my defenses could soon become my strongest assets. Into the wastebasket could go the idea that I was a victim of any of my past—of my parents' hang-ups or of the circumstances which had hurt me. The good Creator made me the way I am for His purpose. If I choose to give myself into His direction, He will make me whole and useful according to His plan.

Becoming the whole person God designed is not a quick and easy operation. I am still much aware of the habits of living that over fifty years of time have helped me form. I have asked for the healing of the original hurt and have received it. On the other hand, I now have the job of *consciously battling* against the habits I have developed to compensate for those hurts. When the sore is well, we no longer need to protect it. But just as a dog will often run on three legs for months after his fourth is healed from an injury, I continue to limp when I no longer need to.

There are ever so many entrances to the side road that leads to depression. I look at them occasionally with longing, knowing that depression is sometimes more comfortable than bright light. But I know, too, that I do not want to waste the joyous music, skipping along the yellow brick road with Jesus toward the wholeness God created for me before the world began.

Scripture

" . . . make Yahweh your only joy and he will give you what your heart desires" (Ps. 37:4).

"God, you are my God, I am seeking you, my soul is thirsting for you, my flesh is longing for you, a land parched, weary and waterless; I long to gaze on you in the sanctuary, and to see your power and glory" (Ps. 63:1-2).

"Return to me and I will return to you, says Yahweh Sabaoth." (Mal. 3:7b).

"Set your hearts on his kingdom first and on his righteousness, and all these other things will be given to you as well" (Matt. 6:34).

"Jesus said to him, 'Go; your faith has saved you.' And immediately his sight returned and he followed him along the road" (Mark 10:52).

"You see, God's grace has been revealed, and it has made salvation possible for the whole human race and taught us that what we have to do is to give up everything that does not lead to God" (Titus 2:12).

"I know, too, that you have patience, and have suffered for my name without growing tired. Nevertheless, I have this complaint to make: you have less love now than you used to. Think where you were before you fell; repent and do as you used to do at first, or else, if you will not repent, I shall come and take your lampstand from its place" (Rev. 2:3-5).

Chapter 11

Giving Up the Costumes

What is Christian behavior?

The wholeness our prayer team is beginning to experience gives us all new freedom. One of the ways that we notice this freedom is in our awareness of the unifying effect of knowing Jesus. Any of us who have met Him in a personal way no longer need to feel defensive toward others whose ideas differ from ours. One of our group is a professional counsellor who often listens to young people express their prejudices and their fears in regard to Christianity. Fear always forms the basis of prejudice, in one way or another; and one of the most obvious indications of prejudice is anger. So she is used to hearing anger voiced toward "Christians." Professional counsellors are not supposed to deal with people in a specifically "religious" sense, but nobody has ever told Nancy not to pray—and she does constantly. As a result, I suppose, the spiritual aspects of life are continually being brought up by her counselees. Through her we have become aware of how often people's preconceived ideas about Christians limit the action that they will allow God to take in their own lives.

I have heard the theme, myself, many times: "I won't be a Christian because some specific Christian does things that are 'wrong.' If that is being a Christian, then I don't want any of it." Admittedly, that Christian has a responsibility to his Lord; so if he is behaving badly, it hurts the Master. But under questioning, the phrases "doing wrong things" and "behaving badly" often turn out to have purely personal connotations and have nothing much to do with a particular person who really knows Jesus.

In some communities, "a good Christian" doesn't dance or smoke or drink. In others he isn't lazy. In some he dares not be unconventional; and if he speaks in tongues, he is an outcast. While in some others, one who attends Mass and has a statue in his church is damned for sure. One church forbids a behavior that another church embraces.

Many limiting prejudices are born out of the fear of someone else whose behavior is different. Living a good Christian life, which is so surely proof of one's holiness, is defined so many ways that to live all of them would be impossible. There is confusion and sorrow and broken hearts, as well, without mentioning such things as the wars which have been fought and the people who have been put to death in the name of living as a good Christian should.

So how should a Christian act? I had to deal with that question one day, and there was no time to do homework. I was in a group of assorted people gathered in an attempt to find a suitable study for regular Sunday morning meetings. Nobody wanted to lead and nobody had an idea that interested more than a small part of the group. There was one girl of perhaps eighteen who wanted a Bible study. She said, in passing, that she could never find any Christians to have fellowship with and she really missed them. The whole group jumped on her as if she had uttered blasphemy.

"This is a Christian community," they pointed out emphatically. "Most of the people around you are Christians. Look at . . ." and they named several names. "Those people live wonderful Christian lives and you are with them every day." The girl shook her head.

"No, I mean *really* Christians," she said quietly.

Everyone's anger surged at once. Who did she think SHE was? Was she so much better than all those other folks they'd mentioned? If *those* people weren't Christians, then they probably weren't either! Prejudices hung out all over the room. The girl, younger and more vulnerable than the rest, retreated in tears. How I wanted to confront the group in her defense! I knew from my own experience the distinction she was trying to identify. I knew her longing to share the love of Jesus in a joyful, uninhibited, non-judgmental conversation without the kind of deliberate intellectualism that would allow Him to come only brain-deep. Somehow, though, it was a day—or perhaps a group—that managed to stop my brain from functioning. If I were to have any part in rescuing Leana from the moment of disillusion and turn it into growth instead, I would have to get out of the way and allow the Spirit to take over. Please, dear Lord, turn this situation into a learning experience in the school of compassion.

* * * * *

When Paul originally called the believers in Jesus Christ "Christians," he was refering only to the ones who had accepted Him into their hearts and their lives completely enough to be willing to live for Him or to die for Him with equal fervor. Knowing Jesus in a personal way was the *only* criterion for being called Christians. In the early beginnings of Christianity, the new converts were a motley assortment. Some had been temple worshipers in the temple of Diana. Some were Greeks, some were Asians, some were strict Jews. They had practically nothing in common—only the one person in their hearts: the Lord Jesus. In many instances, to acknowledge Him meant sure persecution or death. It took courage to say, "I am a Christian," and it often was an act of condemnation to say of someone else, "He is one, too." For that reason, it was a special privilege to be part of the group who used the sign of the fish.

Right away, of course, styles of behavior began to take form, often to fit the character of the community much more than to fit the adoration of the Lord. These community styles still get mixed up with being "Christian," to the point that as soon as a person accepts Christ, he is automatically forced to adopt the local specification sheet. By his careful following of those community rules, he is known. Some new converts, of course, can't stand such pressure and either leave the community or the religion. Others become like the scribes and Pharisees, to whom Jesus had to speak so harshly, and adopt with great enthusiasm whatever existing mores give them the greatest sense of righteousness.

To get out of the trap of this kind of box-around-God, we must ask ourselves if we can see what Jesus himself wanted from us as appropriate behavior. If we can find that answer, then we will have taken a step toward the life which is Christlike.

To begin with, Jesus calls us to a whole new approach to life. It is as if He has taken off our robes of pretext. We might know the choir member in the church because he wears a choir robe. The Altar boys have their own garments. Band members and bus boys and Boy Scouts and waitresses wear uniforms. This outward clothing is what one assumes when he joins the group for which they are the usual costume. Jesus does *not* make such a distinction. When we join forces with Him, it is as if He takes away all of our clothing and starts with our utter nakedness. "No outward show," He tells us. "Whatever is in the heart is the matter of importance." Giving up one's garb is really a freeing experience. Once handed over to the Master, it becomes no longer our responsibility. It is up to Him to dispose of it.

In giving up all of our costumes, though, we are also exposing ourselves to a new openness and vulnerability. Instead of the vestments of our faith, we must have something else more important. Therein lies the special something that Leana was asking for when she said she missed the fellowship of other Christians. Believers in the Lord Jesus have a certain distinct characteristic: they love Him more than they love anything else. Although they still have their humanness and the problems that have come with the flesh, they still have the sure knowledge that He has gone inside and will gradually make them over into likenesses of himself. This sets them apart from their previous natures with a special hope for the future. People who are desperately "living the good Christian life" by their own efforts and without such safe assurance are often troubled and threatened by the feeling believers have for one another. Since part of wholeness is to accept what we consider our inadequacies and deliberately hand them over to Jesus, true believers are often more honest about their own shortcomings than those who have never met the acceptance and forgiveness of God shown through His Son. This honesty is what Jesus asks for when He takes our lives into His hands. All that believers are required to do is believe. Jesus does all the rest. He encourages our cooperation, but in the end what happens is His holy doing. That is a humbling thought—too much to bear unless one has had the personal assurance which comes directly from the Lord.

The interesting thing about this approach to living naked, so to speak, is that our outward behavior gradually changes. If we are continually seeking first Him and His kingdom and not concentrating on our own behavior, we wake up to the realization that our old behavior has changed. It has changed because its focus has shifted from "me" to "Him." However much a man tries to "live a good Christian life" without Christ, he succeeds only in wearing an outfit which covers his outside and does not change his inner world.

Then do Christians think they are better than other people? In some ways they might be said to, and in some ways they certainly don't. Anybody who has met the perfection of God in Jesus Christ is immediately innundated with the knowledge that He is so much more than we are that there is no comparison. In light of the great gap between us and Him, nobody ends up better or worse than anybody else. It is the holy and indescribable miracle that God loves us so much that He bridged the gap between us and himself. Nobody deserves it more than anybody else simply because nobody deserves it at all. Therefore I can never look down on another person, no matter what the circumstances.

But I *can* offer Him the one thing I have which the non-believer has missed: hope. Because of Jesus' death and resurrection, we have ultimate hope, no matter what happens. That is the good news. Each moment is an incarnation and a redemption. Nothing can happen that isn't in the realm of good because of the redemption for which God's only Son laid down His life. Because I have that, I never lose my hope and that hope is the raw material from which my faith keeps growing. If I offer that hope to another person and I am inept or bumbling, shy, out-of-tune with the Spirit, then my offer may come across to him as superiority. It has happened to me and I am truly sorry. It is good to know that no matter how I fall down on the job of living, my Lord and Master can pick up the pieces and fix them, even though I sometimes move too positively with my offer of witness. This is not a costume of Christian living, however. It is an inner conviction which I have not learned to share gracefully. Whoever said that new Christians need to be put in a box with a lid for the first six months was aware of the danger of trying to express joy in terms of the expectations of those who knew that one before the joy arrived. Joy is uncommon country to most of us before we know the Lord's kind. We need to define sensitively the dry-

96

ness of our listeners before we dump too much water on them.

Everyone, though, who has any inclination in the direction of Jesus has one thing in common with all the others: he has made a move, however small, toward the source of life, love and freedom. For all Christians, there is the point of contact. Even if I only call myself a Christian without really deeply believing, at least I am on the edges of the right camp. Therefore all people who call themselves by His name need to practice carefully the love and forgiveness which He taught us.

Sometimes we don't *feel* that love, even among the closest of us. But love is *not* a feeling; love is a *doing*, an action verb. We know He will provide what we ask in the way of unity and understanding. So we ask, again and again. And we *do*, again and again. The corresponding feelings will come.

Christians in church on Sunday may be poor witnesses in their business world, but if they have in any way aligned themselves with the name of Jesus, then some of it will eventually rub off on them because good is stronger and bigger than evil. Whether they know it consciously or not, people are attracted to the power of God's Son. He waits patiently for them to need Him and then He is there. All who call themselves Christians must remember that it is He who chose us from the beginning; and He chose us all. He made us; He wants us; He waits for us.

Our big wastebasket sits waiting to receive our judgment of ourselves and others by the vestment or the uniform—by the outward show of any man. God alone knows what lives in every deepest self.

Scripture

"Know then that Yahweh your God is God indeed, the faithful God who is true to his covenant and his graciousness for a thousand generations toward those who love him and keep his commandments, but who punishes in their own persons those that hate him" (Deut. 7:9).

"For he has not despised or disdained the poor man in his poverty, has not hidden his face from him, but has answered him when he called" (Ps. 22:24).

" 'What I command you is to love one another' " (John 15:17).

" 'But when the Spirit of truth comes, he will lead you to the complete truth' " (John 16:13).

"Your interests, however, are not in the unspiritual, but in the spiritual, since the Spirit of God has made his home in you" (Rom. 8:9).

"It can only be to God's glory, then, for you to treat each other in the same friendly way as Christ treated you" (Rom. 15:7).

"For our knowledge is imperfect and our prophesying is imperfect; but once perfection comes, all imperfect things will disappear" (1 Cor. 13:9).

Chapter 12

John Can't Fix the Vacuum

How does my view of God limit His creative work?

As I have ministered to people through careful listening and inner healing prayer, I have discovered, as I am sure many others have also, that people's feelings about God are very closely connected to their feelings about their earthly fathers. Before wholeness can any more than come into sight on the horizon, it is necessary to deal with that fact. My father was orphaned at three, so he always thought of himself as "a poor little orphan." When he died at the age of nearly eighty, he still regarded himself that way. Of course he was, as a result, often a needy, ineffectual person. He loved as much as he was able, but his own longing for a mother's tenderness and a father's affirmation made him unable to accomplish much in the adult world. I grew up knowing in my intellect that God was all-powerful, but feeling somewhere deep in my insides that when we came right down to, as Mother used to say, "brass tacks," He couldn't do anything for me.

Some parents' insecurities show up as punitive, so their children harbor a God-will-get-me-if-I'm-naughty feeling. Other parents are permissive and uncaring. Sometimes people get their security from being legalists and some from being "good." Hardly anyone I've ever encountered has much gut-level awareness of the powerful love that God has for His children.

How much we unwittingly limit God hit me full in the face one day when I was riding in the car with a group of dear ladies who began discussing a man who had maligned them and hurt their feelings. He had come to apologize to one of the group and she had "accepted his apology."

"But," she said firmly, "God can't use that apology. All he was doing was maintaining his Christian image among his friends. He didn't really repent. God can't use such hypocrisy!"

"God can't?" I thought to myself. "Our all-knowing, all-seeing, all-powerful heavenly Father? From Baalam's ass to Saul on the road to Damascus, God has used impossible, often unhappy or unwilling, subjects. At the same time, He has obviously given us permission to refuse to participate in what He is doing and to hold up God-can't signs in front of our activities. There's some little puzzle here that I'd like to unravel."

The more I thought about it, the more pictures I got of variations on the "God-isn't-able-to-do-it" theme. At that point I (no, I guess the Holy Spirit) started a project that nearly filled the holy wastebasket with my own and my friends' newly discovered blocks to faith. I set about to identify and discard what Thomas Harris calls the tapes playing inside our heads—the God-can't tapes. They were so prevalent that if it hadn't been serious, it would have been funny.

For example, my husband is clever at fixing, building, and rebuilding almost anything. I and our children, plus any number of assorted neighbors, have always brought items which needed repair to him, expecting their rebuilding and almost without fail receiving what we expected. One day I took my vacuum cleaner to him for improvement. He fiddled with it for a bit and then told me that it needed some parts he would have to order. I put it back in the closet unmended. Although he offered to send for the parts, I decided to take it to the repair shop instead. The serviceman fixed it up and presently I retrieved it, working fine. There was no basis for my thinking that my husband could not do the work I needed; but all the same, next time the vacuum cleaner broke, I didn't even ask him. I just took it to the shop. Inside my head, I had a little song that said, "John can't fix vacuum cleaners." My neighbors continued to ask him to repair theirs, and he did without question. My "John can't" was in my own head, not his.

Probably when we act on the assumption that God is unable to do something or other, it is because we ourselves could not do it and could not even imagine *how* God could do it. Or maybe we don't want it done. Would my friend have been truly happy if God had accepted and used the young man's "hypocritical" apology? Wouldn't she have liked it much better if the fellow went for a long period singularly unblessed until, say, he learned his lesson? If she had felt enough inner constraint to turn the problem entirely over to God, she might have found that, like my vacuum cleaner, Father could fix, after all. But she was, instead, limiting God by viewing Him through her own frail image; and He was coming out "can't."

If God could not overcome evil in His world, if He could not turn it around for His own ends, He would never have allowed the angel Lucifer to have had the free choice which permitted him to rebel. Since God created the universe and allowed free choice even among His holy angels, I feel sure He could use what they did, whether we like the idea or not. I do not choose to team up with evil. I do not choose to condone it in my own life. But if I am logical at all, I must admit that God can transform even the worst wickedness into His creative purposes.

We see evidences of "God-can't-because-I-don't-want-to-myself" limitations everywhere we look. I have read in magazines that God can't use psychiatrists because some of them aren't Christian. But I know from experience that many of the truths in psychiatry are scripturally provable and help us to grow in the grace of self-understanding and acceptance. God has used books by eminent non-Christian psychiatrists to effect some of my own deepest inner healing. I have read that God can't use atheists and He can't use educators, and He can't use dancing and He can't use drama; He can't use fat people and He can't use liberals. If all the God-can't people would get together, they would have to laugh at the ineffectual God they have concocted. If I listen even for a moment to the idea of God's inability to repair the brokenness of humanity, I will miss the chance to take my own broken implements to the One who can, indeed, fix them.

Once inspired in my search, I came across another kind of God-can't that I think was more restrictive of growth than the first one. Once my sewing machine broke. I asked my husband to fix it. He tightened this and loosened that, all the time muttering that I hadn't been taking proper care of it. In my emotional immaturity, I was poorly equipped to take criticism, especially when I knew that I had oiled and tightened to the best of my ability. So I became angry. The next time something was out of order in the machine, I quietly took it to the local Mr. Fixit instead of to my husband. It cost me a little money, but at least I was safe from what I felt was unfounded criticism. Was I, perhaps, doing the same thing with God? Was I refusing to ask Him to help me in my places of disrepair because I felt He would blame me— when I felt that I had done the best I knew how all along? It seemed that I had happened onto a deep spot of separation from His living goodness.

No insight ever comes without reason. Immediately other people began to arrive with problems similar to mine. Feeling unsupported and alone, they were afraid God would blame them for their inadequacies. How, Father, can I speak to my friends out of my new understanding? Every time I see one of my old restrictive ideas vanquished, I have a larger awareness of the loving nature of God. Pure love is not punitive, does not condemn, is powerful. Nothing is outside its care and concern. Though none is blameless, nobody is ever discarded by God's abiding love. So He gave me a little love story to share with His children.

*   *   *   *   *

Way back in the beginning when God first created mankind, He put those initial people into a child's-eye picture of heaven. He did it because He wanted them, as they matured, to have a built-in memory of what it was like to be in perfect harmony with Him. That memory has spurred many a person on to a willful choice of the path that leads back to Him. He allowed them to choose to leave Him; but they could never choose not to have known their original destiny. He gave them a blueprint for living. They could forget with their minds, but the truth of God was buried in their subconscious minds. We all know how strong those deeply buried memories are. That knowledge is embedded in the subconscious even though some may claim to have outgrown the need for it.

The blueprint He gave us has since been written down; we have it in hand, the Bible. But God's truth is not always expressed in the loving way it was originally intended to be. People have punished themselves all through the ages; people have hurt themselves and others because of their misunderstanding of the nature of God.

Pretend with me a moment. Pretend that there is a big clean shower room lined with pearl and sparkling with holiness. The faucet overhead is gold. Will you take off all your clothes and go inside? Remove those dress-up outfits that you have been wearing and let your skin be as uncluttered as the day you were born. Then step into the shower. Feel the smooth surface with your bare feet. Can you sense the anticipation? Now turn on the gold shower tap. Warm, sparkling water courses down over your body. It is love. It cools your sunburn and warms your coldness all at the same instant. It dries your tears.

It washes away the dust from the world outside. Soon your whole body is warm and clean, at peace, with love dripping off your nose and the ends of your hair. What satisfaction. You sigh.

But you're not done yet. You reach for a towel to dry your wet hair and to your surprise you discover a little trapdoor in the top of your head. Carefully you pull its handle and open it. Wonder of wonders, your head has a hole in it. Again you stand squarely under the shower and feel the warmth of the clean water—only this time it is running inside you through the hole in your head. You laugh. How ridiculous! Nevertheless, the same joy is filling you, washing the inside as it has just washed the outside. Sin and guilt, fear, unforgiveness, sorrow all flow away under the gush of love that is fast filling up your insides.

You laugh and dance and sing. You fling water around the shower. Nothing has ever happened to you that is as thrilling as this glorious bath. Finally you are as full and dripping as you can be. You turn off the faucet and dry yourself tenderly, hardly able to breathe for the holiness.

But still there is more. After you have dressed in clothes that are suddenly as new as your insides, you remember a person you have always hated. Hated? Yes, you have to admit, there is a person you hate. *No!* There is a person you *used* to hate. Your new center is *free* of hate. As you dry your soft, shiny hair, you have an inspiration. Dressing as fast as you can, you run to find the person and invite her to take a shower in your wonderful new bath. Puzzled and intrigued, she follows you to your house. No matter what went on in the past, she can't resist the love that falls like rain from every part of your body.

You sing as you help her undress and go into the shower. Hate? What's that? As you wait outside, you find yourself making a list of all the people you would like to invite into the shower. You laugh at your tender knowledge that they, too, have trapdoors in the tops of their heads. What a gorgeous secret! The future is full of expectation, and God's world has taken on a new dimension forever in your life.

Scripture

"To Yahweh your God belong indeed heaven and the heaven of heavens, the earth and all it contains; yet it was on your fathers that Yahweh set his heart for love of them, and after them of all the nations chose their descendants, you yourselves, up to the present day" (Deut. 10:14-16).

"I know that you are all-powerful: what you conceive you can perform. I am the man who obscured your designs with my empty-headed words. I have been holding forth on matters I cannot understand, on marvels beyond me and my knowledge" (Job 42:2-3).

"Do you really think I am like you?" (Ps. 50:21b).

"Did you not know? Had you not heard? Yahweh is an everlasting God, he created the boundaries of the earth. He does not grow tired or weary, his understanding is beyond fathoming" (Isa. 40:28).

" 'Who can be saved, then?' they said. Jesus gazed at them. 'For men,' he told them, 'this is impossible; for with God everything is possible' " (Matt. 19:26).

Chapter 13

Golden Parentheses

Is God able to use indirect methods for presenting spiritual truth?

Immediately when I started a housecleaning of God-can'ts, I began finding them everywhere. Sometimes they were in one form and sometimes in another. Many times, I will admit, their real form was, "I don't want God to—." If we don't want God to, He will usually respect our wishes, even when we say with our words that we want something else. He gave us free choice so that when we do choose to come to Him, we might do it, as He said long ago, "with all your heart and with all your soul and with all your strength."

Until I have made contact with my inner self, I cannot willingly give it to Him. If my subconscious is chanting, "No! No! No!" then there is a part of my heart, soul and strength that is not loving God. If I hate my own mother in the depths of my being, then the whole side of

God which the Israelites called Yahweh-Eloihm (Eloihm is the nurturing breast of the caring mother) will not get my love. If I am afraid of gentleness or manliness or anger or any other part of myself, then that aspect of God will miss out on my devotion. When Jesus said, "You shall know the truth and the truth shall set you free," He was explaining the fullest measure of freedom: to love God totally and without restraint.

It takes time for this kind of love for God to develop. It takes, also, our willing participation. That is why I spend a lot of my time praying for the inner healing of people—myself included. Each insight about either myself or someone else shows me, like ripples when a stone hits the water, a bigger and bigger picture of God. God is limitless, but I definitely am not. Sometimes my own limits overwhelm me with smallness. My own limitations become the gap between me and God. Father, forgive me for nurturing my inadequacies in the name of humility. Forgive me for trying to destroy a part of the self which you created in the name of service. Let me, instead, know the real meaning of Jesus' words, "Be ye perfect. . . ."

Several people with whom I fellowship were having an argument about, again, witnessing. We had been discussing books and stories which talked of God in ways that left out all the old terminology.

"Unless the readers know that it is God, Jesus, and the Spirit who cause good, it doesn't accomplish anything to talk about it," someone said emphatically. "We have to tell people the power in the name of Jesus."

Well, I know that. But I felt something amiss in the discussion. So I asked "Why?" Although my question stumped them momentarily, they came up with a perfectly plausable answer.

"Because if we talk about just 'good,' then the humanists and the communists and the pantheists and whoever else we're addressing will think only of themselves and not of God."

"Now I'm stumped," I thought. But still I knew that I was on the track of a God-can't if I could just figure out what it was. I thought of the times I had called upon the name of Jesus and immediately known His presence and help. Could I have called out in the name of just "goodness"? Of course not. The difference is that I know Jesus. Just as I get results by calling "John! John!" to my husband because he knows me and I know him (although I'll admit more people might come if I shouted "John" than "Jesus" in, say, the post office), it is the fact of our personal relationship that makes what I have to say to Jesus in His own name that counts.

"There it is," I said to myself. "We are saying that God can't use the written word to touch our spirits unless we know that we are being touched."

I have often been told by some friend, "You really must meet my pal Joe. He is just the neatest . . ." without feeling the slightest desire to make Joe's acquaintance. She, or someone else, must make meeting Joe in some way intrigue me. My curiosity or my need or my desire to meet him must be stimulated. Even if I have heard of him all my life, I must still have some inner urge to come closer before I will consent to a contrived meeting.

Most everyone in our nation—I dare say most of the

world—has at least heard of God, Jesus, and the Holy Spirit. Sometimes, because of unknown reasons, their very names turn people away from an introduction. Something or someone—of course the Holy Spirit himself, through one channel or another—must break down the barrier. I might go on talking and writing until I die of old age and say "In the name of Jesus" in every paragraph, and nothing would happen. And then again I might write the very word that would spark a longing to "meet this man."

"Don't you think people who don't want to meet Jesus can be tantalized into investigating Him by hints and subtlety?" I asked. Heads began shaking. No, they didn't think God could use "non-Christian" language in which the readers were not specifically made aware of Jesus. We argued long and fruitlessly. God can't. God can't. God can't. Suddenly I hear my own voice speaking.

"I will write a story myself that speaks of the Holy Spirit without using His name or the name of Jesus or even God. Then you'll see what I mean."

Me?

Whatever had I said? Nobody was more surprised at my words than I was. Lord, did I do wrong? Did I speak with horrible pride? Forgive me, Lord, and undo what I have done if you want to. Punish me.

But He didn't undo what I had said. I sat down at the typewriter with no ideas in my head and wrote a story which flowed onto the paper almost without my knowledge. I have read and reread it since, always with surprise at the things my fingers typed on the paper.

GOLDEN PARENTHESES

Phoebe Cranor

I

The morning was as usual as a morning could be. Outside the sunshine was beckoning and inside there was work to do. Margaret shut her eyes for a moment to dim the secret sadness of staying in and shook her head to summon determination for her day's work: dishes and straightening in a hurry and the hole in Ben's nail apron to mend before a meeting of the Morning Fellowship group; and lunch and maybe visitation committee.

"There's too much going on," she thought. "There's never time to do anything right. I'm sick of it." Her eyes reached for the mirror. Yesterday she had looked haggard with smudges under her eyes. Her shoulders had drooped.

"I'm sick of myself. I'm so ugly." It was a recurring feeling and she pushed it down.

"Vanity. Always vanity." She spoke aloud. And in the silence that followed, there was a sound as if someone had touched the edge of a fragile glass goblet with a silver spoon.

"Vanity?" Margaret said again. Again she heard the sound. The cupboard door was ajar and she shut it with a bang. "Vanity?"

The sound of silver-on-glass localized itself in the corner of the shelf where she kept her everyday pottery.

"Pottery goes 'plunk,' " she said sharply, opening the door on the thin sound. Something about the whole incident was becoming threateningly foolish. Nothing *could* be in the shelves with the pottery dishes.

"Good morning, Margaret."

Margaret gasped. Nothing could be in the shelves to speak to her. "Good morning, Margaret?" She slammed the door and returned to the mirror. Her blank stare greeted her. She smiled formally. "Good morning, Margaret." The formal smile looked back at her. She carried the coffee pot to the counter and set it down. She opened the door and took down a mug. A splinter of sound like laughter fell off the shelf and a small glow filled the space where the mug had been. Margaret shut her eyes tightly.

"Strep throat is going around," she said firmly to the empty kitchen.

"I'm so sorry," the glow replied from its spot amid the mugs. "I hope you don't get it." Margaret shook her head again. In the pit of her stomach a coldness solidified. Any idea of illness frightened her. Most of all she feared out-of-control mental rambling. Deliberately she looked at the mugs. She forced herself to focus on the space from which she had moved one. The glow seemed to be gathering and turning. Unbelieving, Margaret saw a tiny personage emerging as if by evaporation in reverse. It was colorful without being colored, musical without sound. Its wings danced with inner light, yet no outline of them was visible. Margaret's lips were dry.

"Wh-wh-what are you?"

"I'm not *what*. I am *who*. I am a fairy."

"That's ridiculous. I don't believe in fairies."

There was another silver sound and the vision moved from the mugs to the counter by the coffee pot. Automatically, Margaret pulled the pot away.

"Don't be silly." Her voice sounded petulant in her empty kitchen. "I have strep throat."

"You need to be beautiful."

Margaret felt a hot spot on each cheek. Who said she needed to be beautiful? Who had the right? "I'm not that bad," she sputtered.

"We're not talking about badness. We're talking about beauty."

Margaret was suddenly very angry. A hard lump of frustration pressed against her breathing.

"All this is perfectly, stupidly ridiculous. I don't believe in fairies and you are not one and you are not here, either." The whole incident was nonsense. Ignoring her thumping heart, she took her coffee and walked into the living room. Bill's boxing gloves lay on the coffee table. Sally's Barbie doll clothes were spread on the sofa. A deep sigh improved her heartbeat, and Margaret set her coffee down.

"There's always too much going on."

II

The house was dirty and Margaret could not clean. The secretary's report was to be done and she could not do it. The Barbie doll still lay on the sofa. In the kitchen was the sound of a silver spoon against a fragile goblet and a glow by the coffee pot. "You need to be beautiful." Indeed?

With a shake of her head, Margaret succumbed. She pulled up a chair and looked at the spot of fragrant light. Its contours formed more solidly and it sat down, too, resting a minúte face against its knees. It smiled.

"I don't believe in fairies, you know," Margaret said. "You will have to prove to me that you are real."

"You see me, don't you?"

"I don't know. Maybe I have a fever and you are a figment of my delirium. Maybe I made you up because I'm bored or have needs not being met by my mode of life. Maybe you are a substitute for my repressed desires."

"Whew!" You must read lots of books." The fairy's voice laughed.

Margaret frowned. "Let me feel of you. If you are real, I will surely be able to feel you." She put out her hand. The fairy shook its head.

"Feeling is just as subject to hallucinations as seeing, don't you think?" Somehow, feeling didn't seem so and Margaret continued to reach toward the little personage. Again it shook its head.

"You don't know my name. Touching is a commitment of personality. I have no personality as long as you are thinking of me as 'it!' "

Margaret was startled. How had, well . . . "it" known how she was thinking? Strangely disturbed, she withdrew her hand. "I won't believe," she thought. But the light still glowed by the coffee pot. The silence became uncomfortable. It was not possible to avoid the inevitable.

"Well, then, what is your name?"

"My name is Beata. Now you may touch me."

Bashfulness overcame Margaret. You cannot touch what you do not believe; yet you must believe to touch. "What would my friends think of all this?" she wondered with part of her mind. "Something is the matter with me," she thought with another. A vision of the deacon's stern wife looking into her kitchen at this moment dissolved the thin control she had mustered to stand guard over her nervousness and she laughed.

"Now do you believe?" Beata asked with a smile more golden than the vapor of her wings. Margaret considered. How could she? No one in her circle of friends would speak to her if she told all this. What good would it do to believe if she could never tell; and if she believed and didn't tell, what good would that be? "No," she thought. "I won't. It would be impossible." But something else inside said, "Believe, Margaret. Do let yourself believe."

"I can't," she said. Beata considered.

"You would have an easier time if you were Sally. She would see me and know me all at once. But I will, if you like, give you a sign. I will make you beautiful." Margaret gasped. That was not possible.

"I will touch you here." Beata left the counter and hovered in the air in front of Margaret. Stretching out her hand, she touched a spot between her breasts where the V of her dress ended and the skin was white. A warm sensation flowed from the spot up into her cheeks and Margaret looked down, strangely, breathlessly embarrassed. The warmth spread upward to her ears, her forehead, her hair. A sound like the music from the big bass pipes in the organ at the church filled herself and the kitchen. And at the same time she was aware of the silver-touching-goblet music that had been there first. She moved to the mirror, her eyes shut, not daring to look.

The glow that was in the mirror was a shimmering rose. Her knees shaking, she let her eyes focus. But the face in front of her was hers. Or was it? It was mixed with the rose and the sound of the fairy until she really did look—yes, she would have to admit—beautiful. And the clock over the mirror said half past nine.

"I must get ready and go to the meeting," she said aloud. "You are not here and I am not beautiful and even though I may be a little feverish, I must go to Morning Fellowship." One had to be a little feverish to speak aloud to a spot by the coffee pot in the middle of the morning.

"I am here and you are beautiful and you will not forget it at Fellowship in spite of the deacon's wife and your milkman's sister." Beata's voice was more firm than her contours. The spot between Margaret's breasts felt as warm as a swallow of hot chocolate. The deacon's wife? The milkman's sister? How did the fairy know about them? Margaret hurried into the bedroom and dressed carefully. As if the mirror were a prying stranger, she avoided it. Finally, shyly, she glanced over her shoulder at her image. There was a murmur of sound and her reflection glowed back at her, surely as lovely as a dream. The spot was glowing.

"I can't believe," she said, "but thanks."

III

"We will have the reading of the minutes." The milkman's sister had a name—Maude Harris. Her mouth was pinched and her nose was sharp. Her voice, too, was sharp. She turned to Margaret.

"Oh . . . the minutes." Margaret felt the smallness of being looked at by Maude Harris overcoming her and she had forgotten the minutes. A long pause followed. Suddenly, at the spot between her breasts where the V of her dress ended—the spot now covered by her small gold locket—she felt a warmness, a rose colored warmness that spread up her neck to her face and her ears and her hair. As she looked at her, Maude Harris' face seemed to be changing. Her mouth was becoming full and soft, her nose less sharp. Her eyes were a strange, lovely shade of grey behind her glasses. Her hair was beginning to shine. She smiled. Margaret smiled back. The distance between them vanished into a sound like the touching of a very thin goblet with a silver spoon. Margaret laughed.

"I forgot them," she said. "I'm sorry. Shall I improvise?" Maude laughed too.

"Better not. Let's just skip it. Minutes aren't so important. Who cares?" Maude Harris was a very lovely person. Margaret tried to reconstruct her old image of the woman, but it would not reappear. She sighed. With a tightly closed hand, she pressed the spot on her neck. Then she looked at the deacon's wife. The deacon's wife had a name, too. It was Eloise Johnston. She was heavily poured into a too-tight girdle and rolling over the top. Her complexion was shiny and her hair too blue. Her voice was filing-a-saw-in-the-basement.

"There is no fairy in my kitchen," Margaret said under her breath and felt the warmness melting under her hand. Looking firmly at Eloise Johnston's too-blue hair, she opened the door and went outside. As she stepped off the curb, she heard a sound of breaking glass. But she hurried on without looking back. Ben would be home for lunch, and it would be reassuring to see him. Things-as-they-used-to-be suddenly became very inviting.

IV

Inside the door, Margaret was shy. Her house, her own house, was filled with strangeness and her own pulse was hammering in her temples. Ben had not come. A shaft of sunshine lay on the rug. Instead of hurrying to the kitchen to fix lunch, Margaret dropped her secretary's books and stretched herself full length in the brightness on the rug. She thought of Maude Harris and her transformation. She felt the warm spot in her breast and she heard the sound of her heart beating.

"I am surely dreaming. I will surely wake up soon," she said aloud.

"Maybe you are awake for the first time."

Margaret shut her eyes for a moment against the glow of Beata floating into the sunshine. Some kind of peace covered her and she lay quiet, allowing joy to swallow her. Then she sat up. Ben would be coming. He would think she had lost her mind. The prospect of his scorn hurried her away from Beata and into the kitchen. And there she stopped with a gasp. The mirror lay shattered on the floor. She remembered the sound of breaking glass as she left the Fellowship meeting, and without knowing how, she knew that she had heard her mirror breaking.

"I do not believe in fairies," she said firmly, going for the broom. "I may be going crazy and we may have had an earthquake, but whatever happens, I do *not* believe in fairies."

"You are being difficult," Beata said from the salt shaker. "I have made you beautiful and you have made Maude Harris beautiful. What more you need, I cannot tell."

"*I* made Maude Harris beautiful?" Margaret looked at the shattered glass in her dustpan. "What did *I* have to do with it?"

Beata reached into the pile of glass and pulled out a piece round and smooth and the size of a dime. She held it up to Margaret. In spite of its size, she could see her whole self in it. As before, she looked at a self which was at the same time her own and more beautiful than her own.

"But why did the mirror break?" Margaret swept the last glass into the dustpan and moved to the trash. Her image in the dime-sized mirror was music in her memory.

"Because of Eloise Johnston."

Ben's step on the porch startled Margaret. She emptied the glass quickly and shut the door. Ben would not notice the missing mirror and he would not hear the sound of a fragile goblet being struck by a silver spoon. But would he see that she was beautiful? The spot was warm between her breasts and she was sure she could hear a distant laugh among the pottery mugs. The tiny mirror lay where Beata had put it by the sugar bowl. "And what if I'm not any different at all?" she thought. "What if I'm only feverish?"

Ben read the mail and washed for lunch. Margaret waited, her hands shaking. The spot glowed, and she felt as bashful as she had on her first date. At last they were eating. Ben finally looked at her.

"Nice outfit you've got on. What you wore to Fellowship?" His eyes caressed her. He never noticed her clothes. It was true. She did look different. Margaret felt a flush rising from her neck to her ears to her hair and the top of her head tingled. Inside the cupboard with the mugs she felt more than heard a sound like the striking of a frail goblet with a silver spoon. She laughed.

"What's funny, Meg?"

"Ben! You haven't called me Meg for—years."

"So? Your name, isn't it?" His expression was a puzzle. Margaret's eyes fell on the tiny mirror. She almost reached for it for a quick look. But surely Ben's expression was enough. She did not need that mirror. Her joy soared.

V

The rest of the day was a surrender to joy and the night was a mist of dreams. But when morning came, Margaret woke with a headache. Inside she felt cold.

"I was getting strep throat after all." She raised herself on one elbow. Ben had gotten up before her and she heard sounds in the kitchen.

Beata. Would he find her? Was she there? Had she ever been there?

"Strep throat's going around," she said dully and got out of bed. But in the kitchen the joy of yesterday came back. The spot between her breasts glowed and the coldness went out of her. Barely waiting until Ben's back was turned, she opened the cupboard and looked at the mugs. Everything in the kitchen seemed to be alive with happiness. The glow was there. The music was there. Beata was there. She fixed breakfast and talked to Ben, got him off to work, fed the children. At last she was alone in the kitchen. Her throat dry, she waited.

"Beata," she called, finally.

"Well, my dear, at last you called me." Beata's form was more lovely than Margaret had remembered. She realized with a start that she had not visualized her at all. Mist and fragrance and sound and glow surrounded her so it was impossible to see her as a single image. Yet here she was again. Suddenly anguish overcame Margaret.

"Do fairies eat and drink?" she asked timidly. Had

she forgotten, in her own preoccupation with beauty, to offer any hospitality to a guest? Where had Beata slept? What had she eaten? Tears filled her eyes and she held out her hands to the tiny personage. "I'm so sorry."

The room seemed full of air and light. The contours of Beata's body and the dancing nothingness of her wings focused more clearly than ever before. With a swoop, she moved from the mugs to the upturned palm of Margaret's hand. There was no sensation at all, yet the warmth of all the colors of the rainbow lay in her palm. She ached to close her hand, to hold forever the tiny form. But she stood, frozen with awareness, holding her breath, not touching the beauty nor moving a finger to trap it.

"Fairies don't need food, but they do need to be fed. I was getting terribly empty, waiting." Tears rolled down Margaret's cheeks.

"I'm sorry. I'm sorry."

The sound of the doorbell shattered the moment. Beata vanished and Margaret wiped her eyes quickly.

VI

At the door, she gasped with astonishment. Her guest was Eloise Johnston with her too-blue hair. Margaret felt herself growing smaller and smaller. The coldness returned to her insides. For a long moment she stood, aware of her old self, afraid of her new one. But as she reached for the doorknob, she felt the tiniest glimmerings of warmth in the spot at the V of her dress where the skin was white. She opened the door with a too-bright smile.

As Eloise seated herself on the sofa, Margaret summoned the warm spot with her will. She felt the nothingness in the palm of her hand and pressed her fingers against it. If Beata were real, she would get her test now. She looked hard at Eloise, waiting.

"Margaret, I have a problem. When I saw how you bewitched Maude Harris, I just said to myself, 'That Margaret is the one to help me.' " Margaret's breath stopped in her throat. *She* had bewitched Maude Harris? She grew again, and the warm spot spread. Maude Harris bewitched! She laughed. Eloise drew up stiffly.

Margaret bubbled, "What a wonderful thing for you to say. I didn't really bewitch her, though, you know. I only suddenly saw that she needed to be loved and it made her beautiful." Margaret was surprised at her words. Was that truly what had happened? She tried to visualize Maude's face as it had been before, but again she found it would not reappear. Eloise was looking at her strangely, her tan eyes asking. "You want that too," Margaret thought, surprised.

"Of course I'll help. What is the problem?"

Two hours later Margaret walked with Eloise to the door. Surely it was only an illusion that they were two lovely ladies, only a dream that Margaret was breathless with anticipation to open the cupboard where the pottery coffee mugs were stacked. She took a deep breath and pressed her hand against her breast. Vanity? Beautiful?

"Beata?"

"Yes, my dear."

"I believe in fairies."

VII

Margaret went to bed warm and elated. She lived the night in the clouds, drenched in moonlight and music. In the morning she could not wait for the daylight and Beata in the cupboard.

"What can I do for her?" she thought. "She has over-turned my life." She thought back over her unbelief and laughed. "I believe in fairies." With a skip she opened the cupboard door. The whole shelf was full of light. She held out her hand and Beata was there, shining. The kitchen was laughing and outside the sunshine sang a gold song on the grass.

"You are very beautiful today, Margaret."

"You did it to me."

"You were ready. Otherwise you would never have seen me."

"Does everyone have a chance to see you? How could that be? Are there others like you?"

Beata laughed.

"Easy now. I can't answer questions. The rules of the fairy kingdom are too hard for people to understand. But I'll tell you one thing: you are more than usually blessed. For you were ready and I was here and our paths crossed like arrows shot from two bows on the opposite sides of the new moon. That happens very seldom, even among the fairies." She sat quiet for a long moment as if in deep thought. Margaret waited, holding her breath. A strangeness came over her, foreboding and dark. She watched as the light glowed from gold to magenta. The shadow of Beata's wings deepened and the edges quiv-ered into blue.

"Fairyland has many rules that even I don't understand." She turned her face up to Margaret. "No fairy must ever stay in one place for more than three days. Today is my last day in your cupboard among your pottery mugs." Margaret gasped. An ache that turned to stone filled her body. The past two days had been so perfect, so joyous. Now, just as she had learned how to know the meaning of happiness, Beata was to disappear.

"Why?" Margaret asked tightly. "You are teaching me to see everyone as beautiful. You make every minute full of anticipation. You make the kitchen a special place. And besides," she drew a deep breath and swallowed the hurting in her throat, "I wasted the first day not believing in you. That day doesn't count." Beata laughed sadly.

"It counts, all right. You are lucky. Most of the people who do see me waste all three days and never believe in me. That is the worst part of all. They are ready to see me and they see me and then they don't believe. That tires me very much." She shook her head and the glow became more purple. Margaret sat in silence, feeling the emptiness of loss as an immovable hardness inside. Never could she be again the person she had been when she awoke that morning. But suddenly Beata laughed.

"Hey! Hey!" she said, exploding into color and movement. "We have the rest of today. And you never know what will happen in a day. Look at Maude. Look at Eloise. And there are many more. Get your pencil. Make a list. After I am gone, you will have more work than you can get done in a hundred lifetimes." Her enthusiasm was contagious. Margaret hurried to the desk, aware of the dissolving of tension. She made a list. She baked a cake. Presently she caught herself singing. Beata darted here and there, sat on the rim of the mixing bowl, tossed golden music like down on everything in the room. The afternoon was long and even and full of deep satisfaction. At last it was sunset.

VIII

Long rays of coral light stretched across the room, past the television which contained Ben and Bill and Sally, and onto the rug before the kitchen door. Margaret reached for the light switch and let her hand fall without touching it. The sunset hour was holy. She held her breath and tasted the flavor of the happiness and sadness and elation of the last three days. Life was enclosing them in parentheses apart from the rest of her existence and yet was the heart, forever afterward, of it. Finally Beata was before her.

"It's time," she said softly. "It's time." Margaret nodded, silent. She felt strangely detached from herself, light and at the same time dark. Beata hovered in front of her. The spot began to glow warmer and warmer. She put her finger against it. Something was there. She looked down, aware of a laugh of joy which sounded like the striking of a clear fragile goblet with a silver spoon.

"It's for you," Beata said. "It's because you believe in fairies." Margaret pressed the dime-sized mirror that suddenly hung from a silver chain around her neck. It covered the spot between her breasts where the V of her dress ended and the skin was white. The back was warm with a clear rainbow of color where it had touched her skin. Carefully she lifted it up and looked in it. Sure enough, she saw herself, the same as before but different as if her every beauty had been touched and all her ugliness forgotten. She smiled at herself and her self smiled back as if they, the two, shared the secret of the universe forever.

"Good-bye, Beata." The shaft of sunshine on the rug dissolved into evening and the kitchen succumbed to the oncoming night. Again Margaret reached for the light switch. As she moved, she felt the firmness of the dime-sized mirror on a silver chain around her neck. She smiled and began to set the table with the pottery dishes from the cupboard.

Scripture

"But I will make the blind walk along the road and lead them along paths. I will turn darkness into light before them and rocky places into level tracks" (Isa. 42:16).

" 'But if you can do anything, have pity on us and help us.' 'If you can?' retorted Jesus. 'Everything is possible for anyone who has faith' " (Mark 9:23).

" 'It is not for you to know times or dates that the Father has decided by his own authority, but you will receive power when the Holy Spirit comes on you, and then you will be my witnesses not only in Jerusalem but throughout Judea and Samaria, and indeed, to the ends of the earth' " (Acts 1:8).

" . . . we have received the Spirit that comes from God, to teach us to understand the gifts that he has given us. Therefore we teach, not in the way in which philosophy is taught, but in the way that the Spirit teaches us: we teach spiritual things spiritually. An unspiritual person is one who does not accept anything of the Spirit of

God: he sees it all as nonsense; it is beyond his understanding because it can only be understood by means of
the Spirit. A spiritual man, on the other hand, is able to
judge the value of everything, and his own value is not to
be judged by other men" (1 Cor. 2:12-16).

Chapter 14

Come Quick! I Think My Pet Dragon Is About To Throw Up

How can we let our faith grow?

This time I had had a new experience. Into my head, instead of a sermon or a story or a parable, came nothing but a title. And what a title! I could hardly believe it. In an effort to be obedient, even when surprises were involved, I wrote the title down: "Come Quick! I Think My Pet Dragon Is About To Throw Up." All day long I pondered on what that title was supposed to mean. Who would I make a speech to, and about what, that would fit such a beginning? I received no ideas whatever. I found out later what my Lord, who has a great sense of humor, was doing; but at the time, I certainly had not the smallest inkling.

Late the following day, I was having a conversation with a man who said what he has repeated regularly ever since I first met him: "I'm from Missouri. I have to be shown." He said it proudly. A little bell began to ring in the back of my head (since I was still on the trail of "God can'ts"). I knew at once that somewhere in this man's Missouri was a new picture of God-isn't-able for my wastebasket, and maybe eventually for his too.

Our inner healing team has prayed many times for the wives and husbands of "Missourians" but never once has one asked for prayer himself. The kind of "showing" the Holy Spirit usually performs apparently doesn't fit into the "from-Missouri" philosophy. In order to be shown, a person has to have his eyes open. My friend continued talking about not being one of those people who were gullible and out of touch with reality. He was not concerned, he said, about his inner world or anything else that had no meaning in the reality of his life. As I listened to him, I began to see that, though Missouri is a fair and lovely state geographically, spiritually it is arid and barren. The people who are proud of their nonbelief get together and reinforce their negative theologies, all the while standing in the very midst of what looks like evident holiness. Yet I know that many have a streak of unbelief somewhere inside. Faith is God's perfect gift. Why do we not all receive it?

Still pondering that question after my visitor left, I turned on the television. A skater was being interviewed. Asked what he did to perfect this skating, he answered, "Practice, practice, and more practice. I have a natural talent for skating," he went on, "but it wouldn't do a thing for me if I didn't spend ten to fourteen hours a day practicing."

Ding went that little bell inside my head. God *could* give that beautiful young man his skating all perfected and ready to perform. But He chose to allow the fellow to participate in his own creative success by doing his part. I could clearly see that he was valuing his blue ribbons more for the work he had put in and the pay-off that resulted than solely for the talent he had naturally. Here was a full-fledged God-can't for the wastebasket. It was not that God couldn't make a perfect skater of the boy. It was, instead, that He chose not to make puppets of His children but to allow them the freedom to decide what to do with their lives in the context of the circumstances of their births. He did not decide to give the skater perfect skating because to do so would be to deprive him of the chance to be co-creator with God in a piece of human raw material.

As I carefully deposited this new God-can't insight in the basket, I realized that this was merely a thin thread of the material my Teacher was giving me a lesson about. I thought again of my friend from Missouri. If God gave the skater a talent but refused to perfect it for him, perhaps He had given all of us a capacity for believing and then left it up to us to develop that capacity. Just as any normal person can probably learn to skate, whether he has a great deal of talent or not, maybe any normal person could learn faith even if he could not necessarily become another St. Paul in the process. Could one really *practice* faith?

I thought about Brother Lawrence of 1666 A.D. and his faith in the midst of a kitchen full of hateful dirty pots and pans. I thought about Frank Laubach and his "each one teach one" philosophy which has so spread knowledge abroad. Those people practiced. They made an effort to develop a talent that they had (or perhaps they didn't have it until they began to practice. Who knows?). Their daily exercise of faith brought about a daily exercise of love because the two seem to be linked together by a holy line. Those men began to see evidence of the results of their believing. Their "show me" was being answered, not with one out-of-the-ordinary miracle but with a day-by-day change in the direction of their own lives and the world as well. Their being shown was connected to their personal choice of direction and their continuous walking in that chosen direction.

Suddenly I realized what that strange title I had received unbidden and could not get rid of was all about. It was a practice chart for daily exercises in faith and love. If somebody were to shout to me, "Come quick! I think my pet dragon is about to throw up," I would have several reactions, each of which could be found more than once in the day of almost anybody. What would I do with my reactions? How would I practice faith and love in each of the hinted situations?

"Come quick!" is an imperative command. My dominated background gives me several built-in responses to being commanded. First, I am angry that my feelings have not been consulted and that I am at the beck and call of anyone who says I am needed. Second, I am tempted not to do what I was told, but, third, I go ahead and do it because I am afraid of making somebody angry with me. Then I feel put-upon and quite likely sorry for myself. All that is an old response which *was* built in by my background but is *now* healed by the presence of the Lord Jesus. Nevertheless, it is still at times a habit of behavior. Am I willing to stretch my faith enough to accept that my reaction is only a habit and that I may now choose to be helpful and loving because I want to? Can I take into consideration the fact that the person who called might very well be going to impose on me and can I laugh about it, still taking the risk that God's love will flow through to that person and to me, also, in spite of it? Can I trust that when I gave my life to the Lord, He will guide it into good, no matter what the circumstances?

"I think . . ." Here is a person calling who doesn't even know what is needed. By the tone of the cry I am asked for more than just my physical arrival on the scene. A feeling is expressed instead of merely a fact: "I feel helpless. I think there is something I need, but I'm not sure what." Can I exercise my caring enough to go to that one without knowing what is really involved? Can I open my lips for the words of the Spirit and trust that those words which I hear coming out are the ones necessary, no matter how they sound to me? It is much easier to say, "If *you* don't know, then how can *I* help you?" and be on my way to more interesting occupations.

" . . . my pet dragon . . ." Heavens! The person who called me is totally out of touch with reality, hallucinating. I don't know anything about such people. I'd better get myself out of here before I'm in over my head. Such would be a very normal response to this cry. Do I dare believe that, even if this person is not mentally on the same track that I am, I can pray with and love and trust God to do whatever is needed through me? Can I stretch my faith enough to see a lovely creature of God behind the ugly cry of a demented mind? Do I dare run the risk to my dignity of associating before my friends with someone who is obviously "off the rocker"? That is an exercise of faith that many of us are not able to complete. It is easier to judge and decide that this one, at least, should go somewhere else for help and love.

" . . . is about to . . . " Nothing has happened yet. Fear of the future and imagined ills not even real are plaguing the person who called me. I surely have better things to do than deal with something which is very unlikely to happen. The world is full of real tragedy. Why bother with some vague kind of worry? Why? Because I myself have always been terribly afraid. I have never been sure the future holds good for me because I was raised a pessimist. I am petrified at the prospect of confronting someone else's unreasonable fears. I feel that I must get away before all my own buried terrors are uncovered. So do I have faith, then, to remember that I have asked a good and loving Father to heal my pessimism and to be present where I have been afraid in the past? Do I have faith? Probably not; but I can practice and develop a little more all the time by responding to the fact that I have asked for freedom from fear of the future, from pessimism and negative thinking. I can communicate love to another faithless person in the bondage of pessimistic future expectations and in the process feel more love and faith in my own life. If I were a skater, I would have to get up off the ice and go again after a fall. I can develop my strength by once again confronting my own pessimism and declaring that it *is* healed.

" . . . about to throw up." This one is the last straw! Must I be involved in made-up ugliness of the most repulsive sort? I am afraid I will throw up, too. I can't minister to someone else's sickness without falling back into my own trough of inadequacies. So I must again practice my own faith, even in the face of a crack in the ice, and reach out to the person with a problem that is "only in the imagination," knowing that God will fix this one's imagination right along with the soul and spirit and skinned knee. I must go a little bit beyond my own capacities all the time, just as the athlete does, in order to strengthen my muscles of faith. When I do, I see results. The person who called to me is better. The little day-to-day activities don't cause the dragon to throw up, and the dragon's owner can finally get himself a real life instead of one concocted out of purple nothingness. I have "seen" the result of faith. I have been shown. But if I had sat around doubting my beliefs and then enthusiastically believing my doubts, I would not have been able to see any results at all.

"Show me," my friend from Missouri would say, and I could never show him. He wouldn't hear the little story about the dragon. He wouldn't see the tiny miracles. He had his eyes closed, his faith as undeveloped as the ankles of a non-skater.

Scripture

"Raise me up when I am most afraid, I put my trust in you; in God whose word I praise, in God I put my trust, fearing nothing; what can men do to me?" (Ps. 56:3-4).

"But they would not pay attention; they turned a petulant shoulder; they stopped their ears rather than hear; they made their hearts adamant rather than listen to the teaching and the words that Yahweh Sabaoth had sent his spirit through the prophets of the past" (Zech. 7:11-12).

" 'So you are a king then?' said Pilate. 'It is you who say it,' answered Jesus. 'Yes, I am a king. I was born for this, I came into the world for this: to bear witness to the truth; and all who are on the side of truth listen to my voice.' 'Truth?' said Pilate. 'What is that?' " (John 18:37-38).

"Only faith can guarantee the blessings that we hope for, or prove the existence of the realities that at present remain unseen" (Heb. 11:1).

Chapter 15

A Wastebasket Full of Surprises

How can God make positives out of the negatives in my life?

Trying to practice faith in the daily vicissitudes of life, I have learned, is full of challenges and also surprises. One day I was helping a friend prepare for a party. She is short of stature too, and we know there is nothing we can do about it. So when we were faced with a shelf full of party goblets that were far out of our reach, we recognized that we had several choices for getting them. Before we had decided whether to use a chair or go after a ladder, a tall friend came up. Instead of saying, "Here, let me help you," as I had happily expected him to, he leaned against the counter, a twinkle in his eye, and intoned piously, "Well, there's only one answer to your problem. You'll just have to be tall." Instead of laughing at him, I found myself hot and shaking with unexpected anger. I was furious. I wanted to hit him with a goblet, if I could have gotten one. And as soon as I recognized my anger, I was also overcome with guilt and embarrassment. It was a happy, joking time, and suddenly I could not take a joke. I stood with my face red, waiting to see what would happen next.

As the team and I have prayed for the inner healing of old hurts in both ourselves and others, we have come across a helpful tool for focusing our attention on unresolved and untempered pain from past wounds. That tool is anger. Like a sharpened pointer, it aims itself in the direction of something the Lord Jesus is ready and waiting to heal. We have been taught to suppress anger, so sometimes it is hard to acknowledge particularly what seems like unreasonable rage. I turned to my friends in uncomfortable confession and told them the way I was feeling.

"Well, let's get to the bottom of it," they said, setting me on a chair and moving close beside me. As they prayed softly, I relaxed and let myself feel the quiet and peace that the presence of Jesus has waiting if we will just stop and accept it. I began to let my mind go back into my past where the pray-ers were inviting Jesus to touch and remove old hurts. I relived times of stress when my mother had told me, "You know you don't feel that way . . ." or, "You don't *really* want that," or, "Oh, we know that isn't what you really think." And later on when my husband would say to me, "You know you're silly to react that way," I would immediately experience again the terrible defenselessness of having another person define my being. Mother's denial of my unique self left me helpless. That same helplessness became rage whenever any implied that they were telling me how to feel—as, ever so jokingly, my tall friend had copied the "well, you'll just have to have faith," which has always triggered my anger.

The pain of that long-age negation of the real me was suddenly unbearable. I willingly opened myself to healing, visualizing Jesus as He went back into those hurting times in my life and affirmed the rightness of my feelings, thoughts, wants: all the realities of me-as-I-am whom God created because He loved me. I relived the anger and frustration as I saw my Lord touching them; and warmth poured over me like golden honey. I knew that He had in truth gone to the source of much of my later pain. I knew, also, that He would help me day by day to break the habits of reacting as I had always reacted. It was a lovely, holy moment. As I sat enjoying it, I had a surprise. Into my already in-tune imagination came the dear old wastebasket. It circled around the table and then floated down in front of me. I began to prepare myself for a discard; but, to my surprise, I saw that the basket was already full. Not only that, it was full of beautifully wrapped packages tied with colorful bows. They sparkled and shone with nothing less than heavenly light. I gasped.

"Redemption didn't just happen once," I seemed to hear a voice saying. "It happens every day, every hour, even every second." Redemption was the giving of His life by Jesus, Son of God, for the sins of the world. Redemption restored my relationship with God, the Creator, and let me, again, as in the Garden of Eden, call Him Daddy. God had taken the trash from my life and turned it into beauties beyond my fondest dreams.

I reached for a package to untie, trembling with

Christmas anticipation. The first one I opened was my lonely, restricted childhood under the constant supervision of my mother, with my father helpless to rescue me from what seemed like an impossible prison. It had changed, not so much as to be unrecognizable but enough that it suddenly looked beautiful. I saw that I had turned for comfort and friendship to the God who said, "If you truly look for me, you will surely find me," to the Jesus who said, "Seek and you will find," to the Spirit about whom Jesus said, "I will send you a Comforter." I breathed a "thank-you" and reached expectantly for the next gift.

My second gift was a year spent in bed, restrained from moving even my arms. It had been a time of great frustration and mental and emotional pain for a child only eight years old. Now I saw the gift of that year: a period of time for the extensive development of a fertile imagination. I created a world of color, sound, music, poetry. I learned to play with companions who were, I can now tell, divine playmates sent by the Lord to keep me from being alone.

The next gift was tied to that one with a silver ribbon. It was the monetary poverty which kept our acquisition of books at a meager level so that after I had read and reread what we had, I spent long and particularly happy hours playing in the big dictionary. I would trace rows of synonyms to see how many I could line up that said the same thing. Then I would trace them to see how far from the original meaning I could make them lead. I made them into families and gave them colors, tunes, shapes. I grouped them in rhymes. I made quilt patterns out of their designs. Those words were a gift from God that, given back to Him, make it possible for me now to write and speak to people in whatever form of our language they can understand.

My next gift had purple paper, but somehow it shone with such a bright glow that I opened it tenderly. It was a broken neck I suffered when I was six but didn't discover until I was past fifty. All the years that I experienced degrees of pain, thinking it was the natural human condition, were suddenly before me as the gift of opportunity (and means) to find happiness over and above pain—to be productive anyhow and to be sensitive to others' pain as well. Thank you, Lord that you redeemed the piano practicing, sewing, writing, studying, skating, biking when it hurt, into a gift of your love that is more real than any pain has ever been.

The ache of retarded emotional development was also a dreary package until I saw that it had grown up to be a tremendous empathy with and love for not only children as such but also a sensitivity to the hurting and needy child who often lives in another adult. I am frequently the first one in our team to feel the pain of that sad child and hunt it out for prayer.

Living close to people whom I love who stubbornly refuse to acknowledge Father, Son and Holy Spirit has seemed, sometimes, like an unbearable sorrow. This gift was in the basket, too, in paper splashed with a thousand flowers. For years I have practiced using the words and the imagination, the logic that God endowed me with, and all the parables I can imagine, to try to reach their needing spots with the "Good News." And in so doing, I have spoken and written to people all over the country with words that God has given them through me. He has let me have this joyous way of glorifying Him with all my might—and all because of what has seemed to me to be a dismal failure in my life.

God has been gradually removing the things that I used to be dependent upon and substituting himself. It isn't finished yet. I catch a dependency every little while: reputation, security, activity, feelings, friends. But each time I see one, I am sure all over again that if I lost it, I would do the only thing I have ever known to do: turn to Him.

The wastebasket is still here, empty of obvious gifts and waiting for more old trash that is keeping me from seeing aspects of my Lord that He would like for me to see. I notice that there is something right now I must put in. It is an old misconception that says, "People don't change. Circumstances do and cultures do and the weather does, but a person is always the way he began." I see that idea as a limitation, even though I also see it as the skeleton of a truth. We are created unique, and each of us has those characteristics which our loving Father gave us before the world began. These are ours and they don't change. But as they develop and come up from hiding, healed from their scars and made whole with the love of Jesus shining on them, they look different. His light is like the prism in my window. It shows us for what we are: a rainbow of beautiful differences melded into a unity. Now we see through a glass darkly, but some day we'll find out how it all really is. Someday we'll recognize ourselves and those around us as bits of a great wholeness—that can be spelled "h-o-l-i-n-e-s-s" just as well. "Be whole," said our Lord. "Be holy!" The wastebasket is beginning to show me what Paul was telling us when he said, "Be happy at all times; pray constantly, and for all things give thanks to God because this is what God expects you to do in Christ Jesus" (1 Thess. 5:17). He was telling us that with Jesus, all things are possible; that hidden in every problem is a beautiful gift from God.

Scripture

"Yahweh your God has blessed you in all you do; he has watched over your journeying through this vast wilderness. Yahweh your God has been with you these forty years and you have never been in want" (Deut. 2:7).

"But I for my part rely on your love, Yahweh; let my heart rejoice in your saving help. Let me sing to Yahweh for the goodness he has shown me" (Ps. 13:5).

"It was good for me to have to suffer, the better to learn your statutes . . . I know that your rulings are righteous, Yahweh, that you make me suffer out of faithfulness. Now, please let your love comfort me, as you have promised your servant" (Ps. 119:71, 75-76).

"I will give glory to you all the years of my life for my sufferings. Lord, my heart will live for you alone. You will cure me and give me life, my suffering will turn to health" (Isa. 38:15b-17).

" 'I will make up to you for the years devoured by grown locust and hopper by shearer and young locust, my great army which I sent to invade you.' You will eat to your heart's content, will eat your fill and praise the name of Yahweh your God who has treated you so wonderfully. (My people will not be disappointed any more.)" (Joel 2:25-26).

142

" 'I have come so that they may have life and have it to the full' " (John 10:10).

" 'We all have to experience many hardships,' they said, 'before we enter the kingdom of God.' " (Acts 14:22).

"Happy the man who stands firm when trials come. He has proved himself, and will win the prize of life, the crown that the Lord has promised to those who love him" (James 1:12).

Index of Scripture

Chapter I

Psalm 18:16b-17; Micah 7:18-19; Luke 4:17-21; Romans 2:1; 2 Corinthians 1:9-11.

Chapter II

Psalm 14:2; Psalm 16:7; Hosea 6:6; John 15:16; Romans 10:3-4; Philippians 1:6.

Chapter III

Isaiah 52:2; Malachai 3:16; Matthew 23:23; Romans 12:2; 2 Corinthians 3:18.

Chapter IV

Genesis 2:25; Psalm 37:5; Song of Songs 8:9b; Mark 2:25-28; Romans 7:6.

Chapter V

Job 33:14; Psalm 19:13; Luke 12:12; 1 Corinthians 3:6.

Chapter VI

Proverbs 19:21; Zephaniah 3:19B; Mark 8:33b; 1 Corinthians 4:1-5

Chapter VII

Ezekiel 12:21-25; Habakkuk 2:1-5; Luke 24:23; 1 Corinthians 15:10; 2 Corinthians 5:17; 2 Corinthians 6:1; 2 Corinthians 12:1; James 4:8.

Chapter VIII

Psalm 22:5; Psalm 33:13-16; Isaiah 65:24; Matthew 21:22; John 6:44; Colossians 3:4; Revelation 5:8.

Chapter IX

1 Samuel 16:7; Psalm 7:15-16; Psalm 13:5; Psalm 85:8-9; Jeremiah 2:19; Jonah 2:9; John 8:51; John 15:9, 10, 12; Galatians 3:13; 2 Peter 2:19b; John 15:2, 9.

Chapter X

Psalm 37:4; Psalm 63:1-2; Malachai 3:7b, Matthew 6:34; Mark 10:52; Titus 2:12; Revelation 2:3-5.

Chapter XI

Deuteronomy 7:9; Psalm 22:24; John 15:17; John 16:13; Romans 8:9; Romans 15:7; 1 Corinthians 13:9.

Chapter XII

Deuteronomy 10:14-16; Job 42:2-3; Psalm 50:21b; Isaiah 40:28; Matthew 19:26.

Chapter XIII

Isaiah 42:16; Mark 9:23; Acts 1:8; 1 Corinthians 2:12-16.

Chapter XIV

Psalm 56:3-4; Zechariah 7:11-12; John 18:37-38; Hebrews 11:1.

Chapter XV

Deuteronomy 2:7; Psalm 13:5; Psalm 119:71, 75-76; Isaiah 38:15b-17; Joel 2:25-26; John 10:10; Acts 14:22; James 1:12.